LEO

ANTARES

EPISODE 4

CINEBOOK
The 9th Art Publisher

Original title: Episode 4

Original edition: © Dargaud Paris, 2011 by LEO
www.dargaud.com
All rights reserved

English translation: © 2013 Cinebook Ltd

Translator: Jerome Saincantin
Lettering and text layout: Patrice Leppert
Printed in Spain by Just Colour Graphic

This edition first published in Great Britain in 2013 by
Cinebook Ltd
56 Beech Avenue
Canterbury, Kent
CT4 7TA
www.cinebook.com

A CIP catalogue record for this book
is available from the British Library

ISBN 978-1-84918-166-2

9th CINEBOOK
The 9th Art Publisher

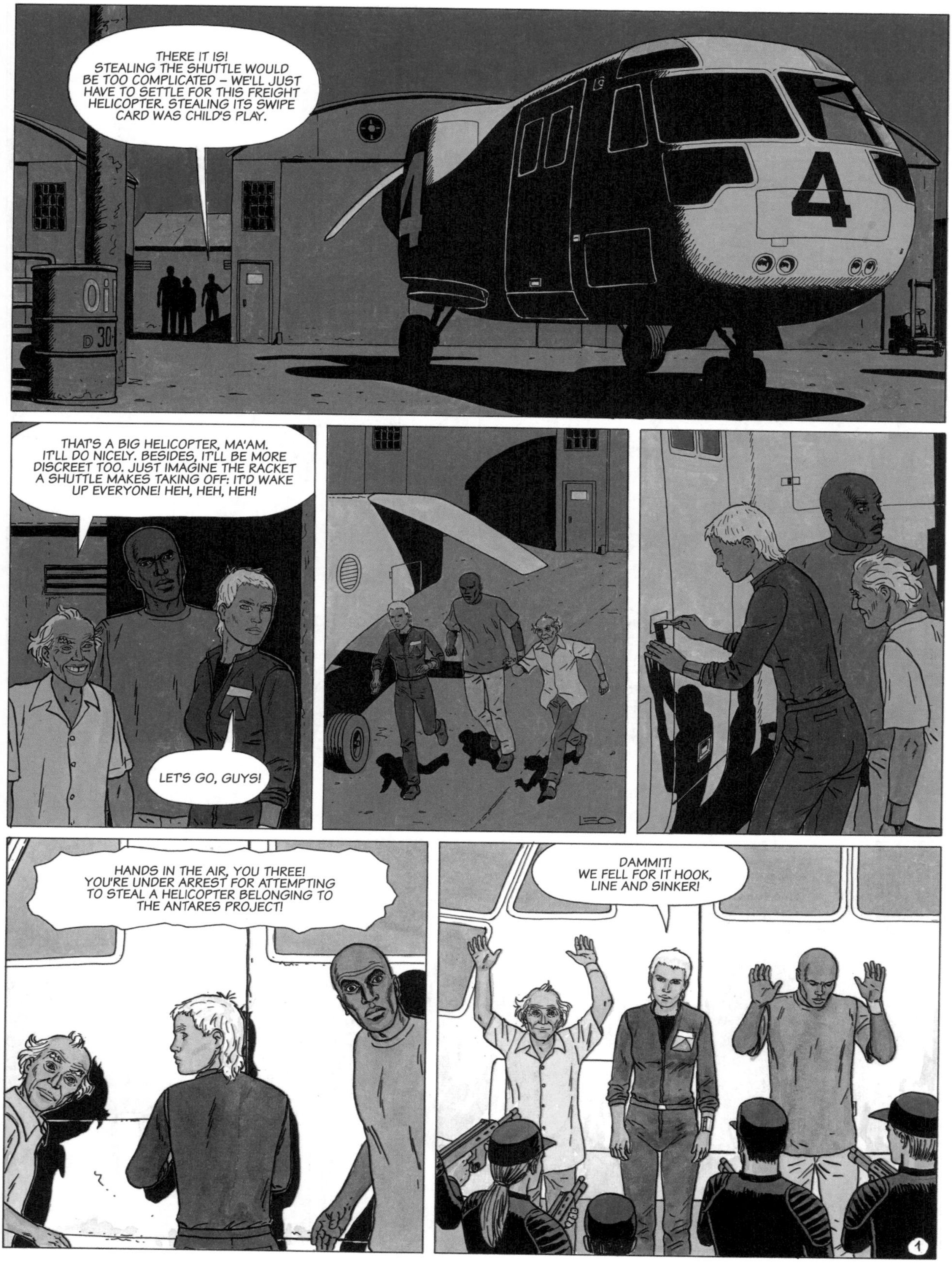

THERE IT IS! STEALING THE SHUTTLE WOULD BE TOO COMPLICATED – WE'LL JUST HAVE TO SETTLE FOR THIS FREIGHT HELICOPTER. STEALING ITS SWIPE CARD WAS CHILD'S PLAY.
Oil
D 30
4
THAT'S A BIG HELICOPTER, MA'AM. IT'LL DO NICELY. BESIDES, IT'LL BE MORE DISCREET TOO. JUST IMAGINE THE RACKET A SHUTTLE MAKES TAKING OFF: IT'D WAKE UP EVERYONE! HEH, HEH, HEH!
LET'S GO, GUYS!
LEO
HANDS IN THE AIR, YOU THREE! YOU'RE UNDER ARREST FOR ATTEMPTING TO STEAL A HELICOPTER BELONGING TO THE ANTARES PROJECT!
DAMMIT! WE FELL FOR IT HOOK, LINE AND SINKER!
1

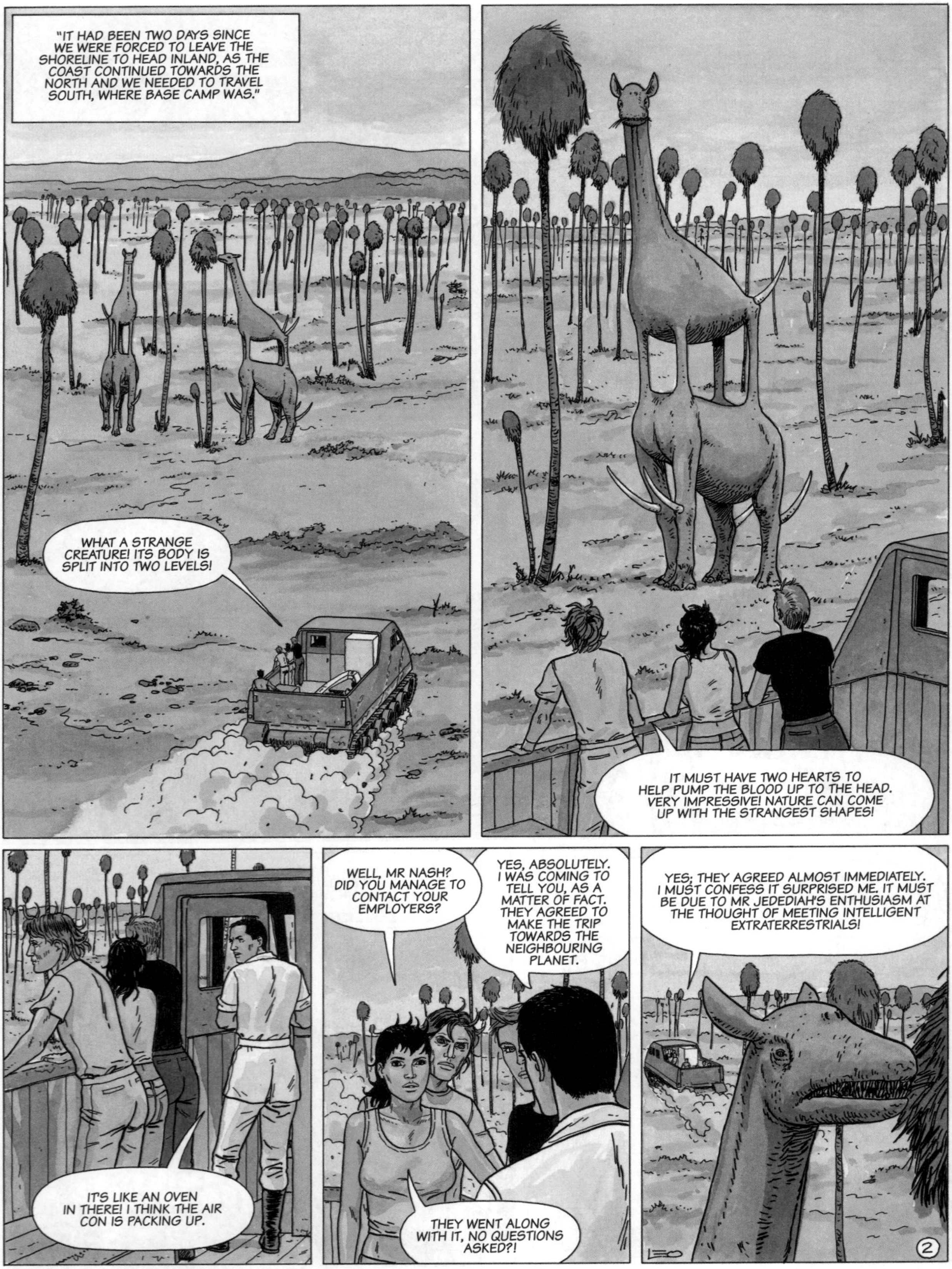
"IT HAD BEEN TWO DAYS SINCE WE WERE FORCED TO LEAVE THE SHORELINE TO HEAD INLAND, AS THE COAST CONTINUED TOWARDS THE NORTH AND WE NEEDED TO TRAVEL SOUTH, WHERE BASE CAMP WAS."
WHAT A STRANGE CREATURE! ITS BODY IS SPLIT INTO TWO LEVELS!
IT MUST HAVE TWO HEARTS TO HELP PUMP THE BLOOD UP TO THE HEAD. VERY IMPRESSIVE! NATURE CAN COME UP WITH THE STRANGEST SHAPES!
IT'S LIKE AN OVEN IN THERE! I THINK THE AIR CON IS PACKING UP.
WELL, MR NASH? DID YOU MANAGE TO CONTACT YOUR EMPLOYERS?
YES, ABSOLUTELY. I WAS COMING TO TELL YOU, AS A MATTER OF FACT. THEY AGREED TO MAKE THE TRIP TOWARDS THE NEIGHBOURING PLANET.
THEY WENT ALONG WITH IT, NO QUESTIONS ASKED?!
YES; THEY AGREED ALMOST IMMEDIATELY. I MUST CONFESS IT SURPRISED ME. IT MUST BE DUE TO MR JEDEDIAH'S ENTHUSIASM AT THE THOUGHT OF MEETING INTELLIGENT EXTRATERRESTRIALS!
LEO
2

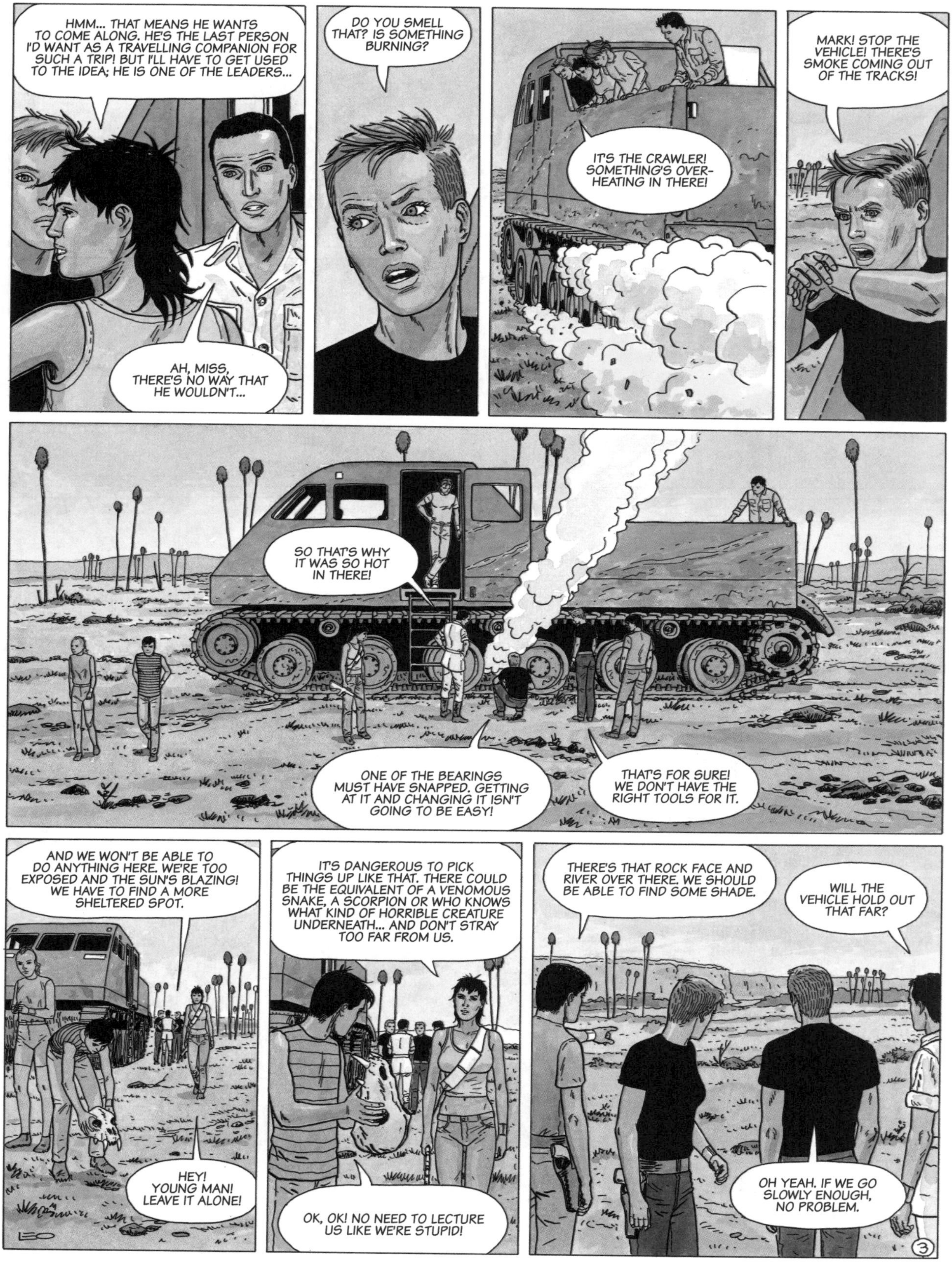
HMM... THAT MEANS HE WANTS TO COME ALONG. HE'S THE LAST PERSON I'D WANT AS A TRAVELLING COMPANION FOR SUCH A TRIP! BUT I'LL HAVE TO GET USED TO THE IDEA; HE IS ONE OF THE LEADERS...
AH, MISS, THERE'S NO WAY THAT HE WOULDN'T...
DO YOU SMELL THAT? IS SOMETHING BURNING?
IT'S THE CRAWLER! SOMETHING'S OVER-HEATING IN THERE!
MARK! STOP THE VEHICLE! THERE'S SMOKE COMING OUT OF THE TRACKS!
SO THAT'S WHY IT WAS SO HOT IN THERE!
ONE OF THE BEARINGS MUST HAVE SNAPPED. GETTING AT IT AND CHANGING IT ISN'T GOING TO BE EASY!
THAT'S FOR SURE! WE DON'T HAVE THE RIGHT TOOLS FOR IT.
AND WE WON'T BE ABLE TO DO ANYTHING HERE. WE'RE TOO EXPOSED AND THE SUN'S BLAZING! WE HAVE TO FIND A MORE SHELTERED SPOT.
HEY! YOUNG MAN! LEAVE IT ALONE!
LEO
IT'S DANGEROUS TO PICK THINGS UP LIKE THAT. THERE COULD BE THE EQUIVALENT OF A VENOMOUS SNAKE, A SCORPION OR WHO KNOWS WHAT KIND OF HORRIBLE CREATURE UNDERNEATH... AND DON'T STRAY TOO FAR FROM US.
OK, OK! NO NEED TO LECTURE US LIKE WE'RE STUPID!
THERE'S THAT ROCK FACE AND RIVER OVER THERE. WE SHOULD BE ABLE TO FIND SOME SHADE.
WILL THE VEHICLE HOLD OUT THAT FAR?
OH YEAH. IF WE GO SLOWLY ENOUGH, NO PROBLEM.
3

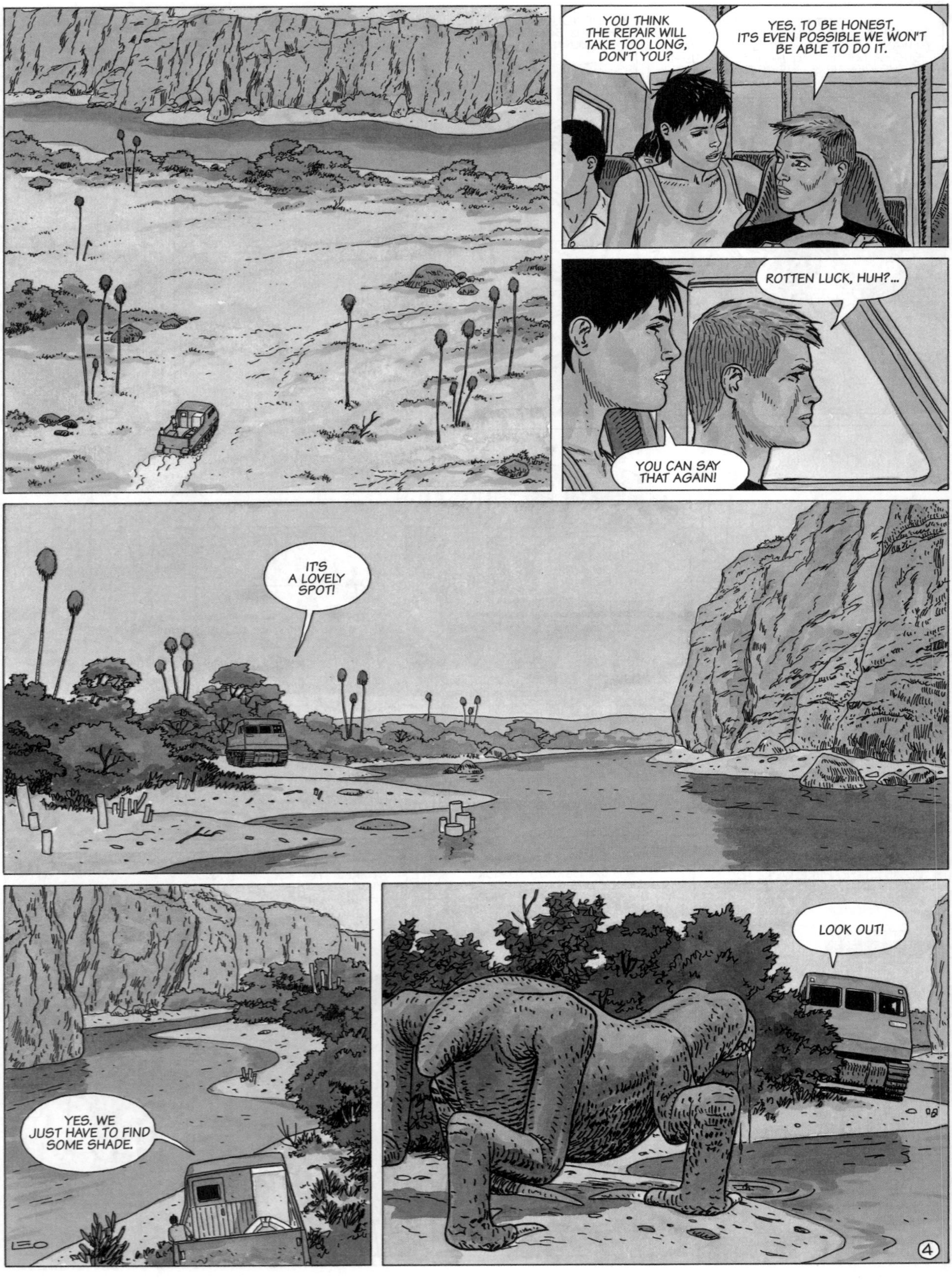
YOU THINK THE REPAIR WILL TAKE TOO LONG, DON'T YOU?
YES. TO BE HONEST, IT'S EVEN POSSIBLE WE WON'T BE ABLE TO DO IT.
ROTTEN LUCK, HUH?...
YOU CAN SAY THAT AGAIN!
IT'S A LOVELY SPOT!
YES. WE JUST HAVE TO FIND SOME SHADE.
LEO
LOOK OUT!
4

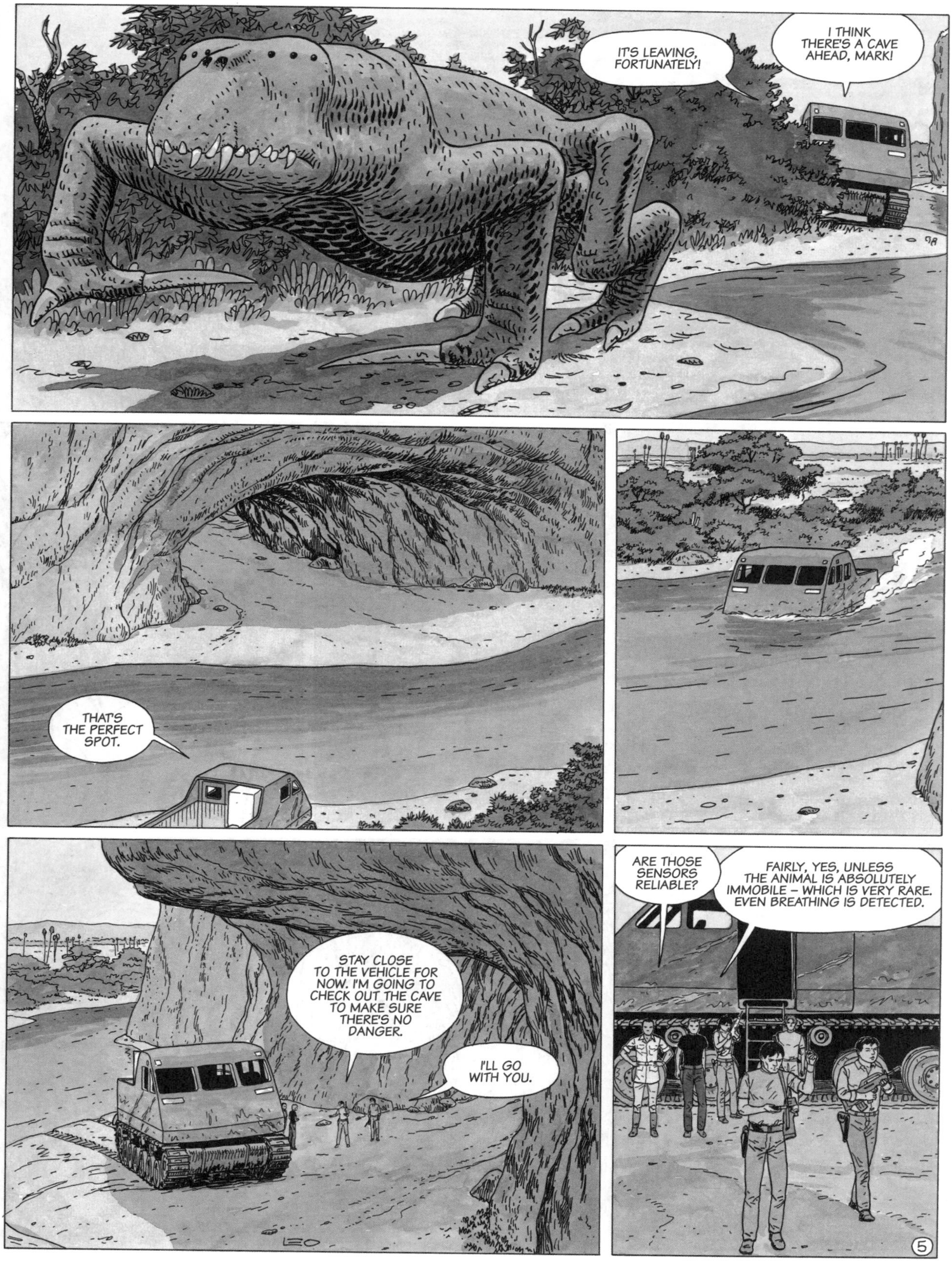
IT'S LEAVING, FORTUNATELY!
I THINK THERE'S A CAVE AHEAD, MARK!
THAT'S THE PERFECT SPOT.
STAY CLOSE TO THE VEHICLE FOR NOW. I'M GOING TO CHECK OUT THE CAVE TO MAKE SURE THERE'S NO DANGER.
I'LL GO WITH YOU.
ARE THOSE SENSORS RELIABLE?
FAIRLY, YES, UNLESS THE ANIMAL IS ABSOLUTELY IMMOBILE – WHICH IS VERY RARE. EVEN BREATHING IS DETECTED.
LEO
5

THERE'S LIGHT OVER THERE, AT THE BACK!

ANOTHER EXIT?

EXPLAIN SOMETHING TO ME, ZAO. ALL YOUR LIFE, YOU'VE BEEN MILITANTLY ANTI-RELIGIOUS, AND HERE YOU ARE WORKING FOR A CULT OF FANATICS. IT MAKES ZERO SENSE!

I GOT TRAPPED, ZHOU, PLAIN AND SIMPLE. I DIDN'T PAY ATTENTION AT FIRST; I JUST WANTED TO GET AWAY FROM EARTH ... FAR AWAY FROM YOU ALL!

BUT DON'T WORRY, I INTEND TO DO SOMETHING...

DO WHAT?! WHAT DO YOU HOPE TO ACCOMPLISH ALONE?

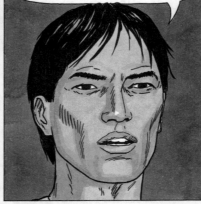

I'M NOT ALONE. TO START WITH, THERE'S KIM KELLER AND HER FRIENDS. THEY'RE GOOD PEOPLE. AND THERE ARE OTHER PEOPLE AMONG THE COLONISTS AND THE CREW WHO AREN'T MEMBERS OF THAT CULT.

BUT I'M CERTAINLY NOT GOING TO USE YOUR VIOLENT METHODS. I DON'T BELIEVE IN VIOLENCE ANY MORE, AS I'VE TOLD YOU A THOUSAND TIMES.

HMM... I DON'T THINK YOU'LL GET ANYWHERE. ACTUALLY, I DON'T THINK THERE'S ANY HOPE LEFT. MY WHOLE GROUP'S BEEN WIPED OUT, AND I'M LEFT ALL ALONE LIKE A DAMN FOOL, NOT EVEN KNOWING WHAT TO DO WITH MYSELF...

AN OPENING! LET'S SEE WHERE IT LEADS.

BE CAREFUL, ZAO! IT'S EASY TO GET CORNERED IN THIS PLACE!...

6

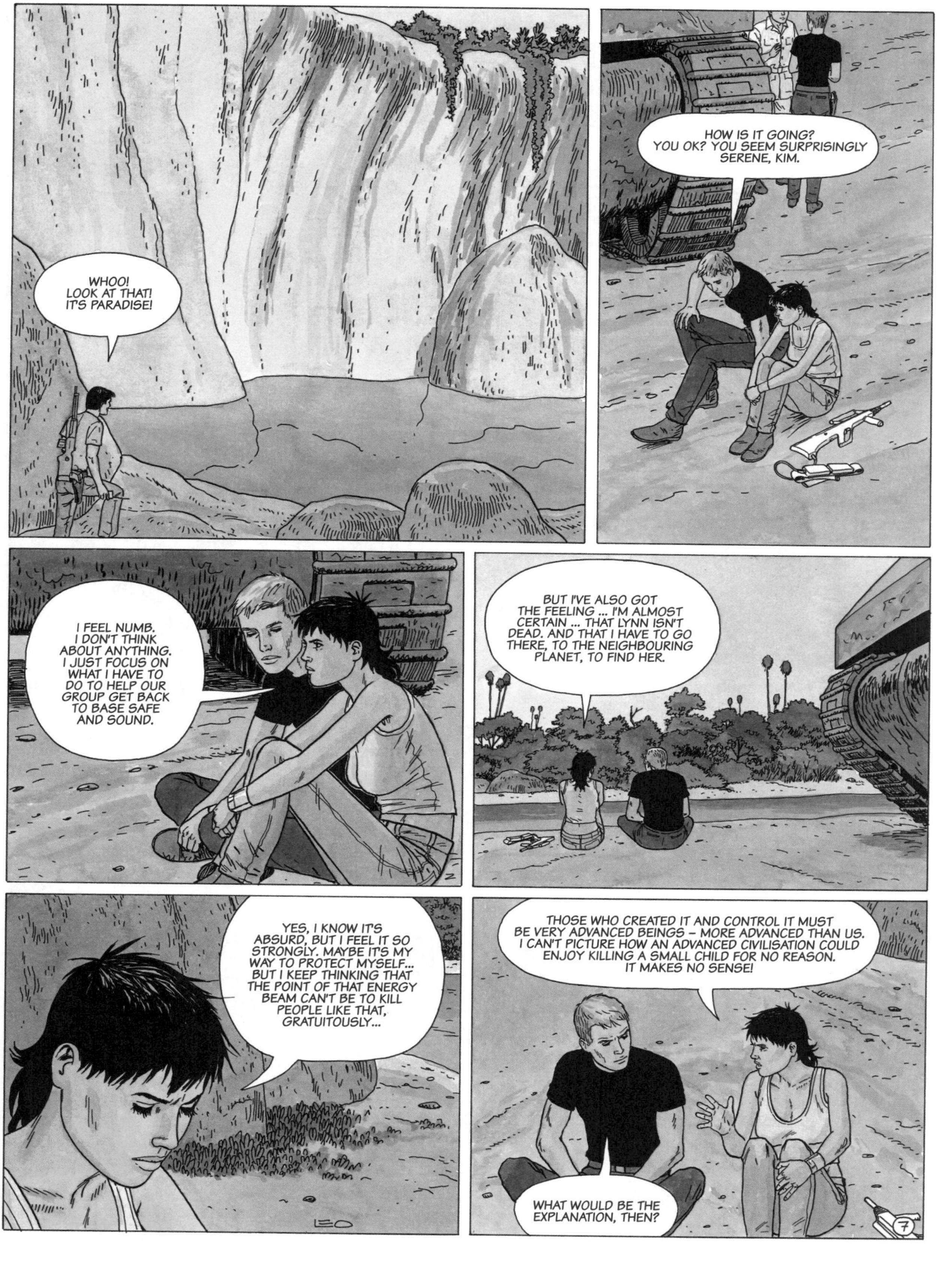
WHOO! LOOK AT THAT! IT'S PARADISE!
HOW IS IT GOING? YOU OK? YOU SEEM SURPRISINGLY SERENE, KIM.
I FEEL NUMB. I DON'T THINK ABOUT ANYTHING. I JUST FOCUS ON WHAT I HAVE TO DO TO HELP OUR GROUP GET BACK TO BASE SAFE AND SOUND.
BUT I'VE ALSO GOT THE FEELING ... I'M ALMOST CERTAIN ... THAT LYNN ISN'T DEAD. AND THAT I HAVE TO GO THERE, TO THE NEIGHBOURING PLANET, TO FIND HER.
YES, I KNOW IT'S ABSURD, BUT I FEEL IT SO STRONGLY. MAYBE IT'S MY WAY TO PROTECT MYSELF... BUT I KEEP THINKING THAT THE POINT OF THAT ENERGY BEAM CAN'T BE TO KILL PEOPLE LIKE THAT, GRATUITOUSLY...
LEO
THOSE WHO CREATED IT AND CONTROL IT MUST BE VERY ADVANCED BEINGS – MORE ADVANCED THAN US. I CAN'T PICTURE HOW AN ADVANCED CIVILISATION COULD ENJOY KILLING A SMALL CHILD FOR NO REASON. IT MAKES NO SENSE!
WHAT WOULD BE THE EXPLANATION, THEN?
7

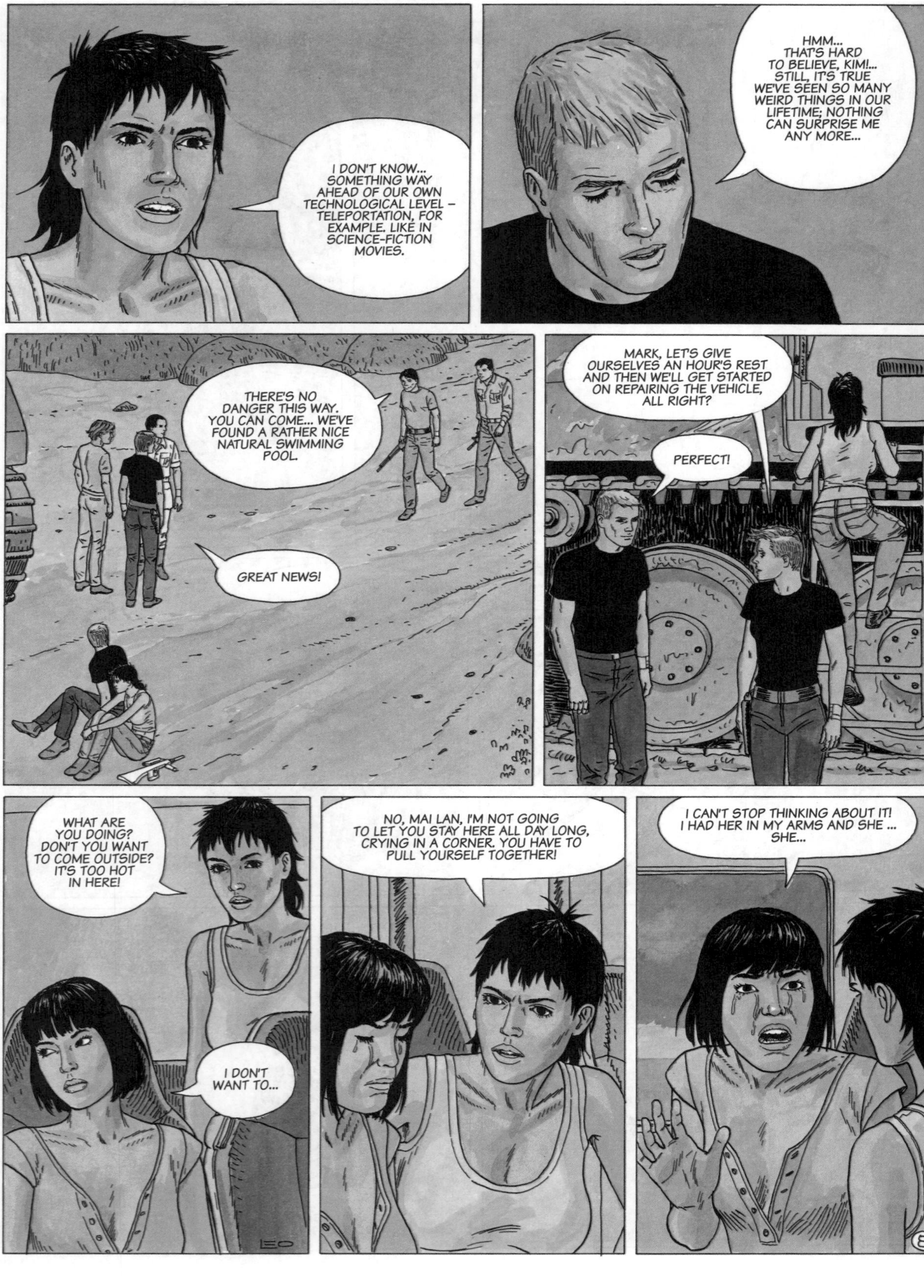
I DON'T KNOW... SOMETHING WAY AHEAD OF OUR OWN TECHNOLOGICAL LEVEL – TELEPORTATION, FOR EXAMPLE. LIKE IN SCIENCE-FICTION MOVIES.
HMM... THAT'S HARD TO BELIEVE, KIM!... STILL, IT'S TRUE WE'VE SEEN SO MANY WEIRD THINGS IN OUR LIFETIME; NOTHING CAN SURPRISE ME ANY MORE...
THERE'S NO DANGER THIS WAY. YOU CAN COME... WE'VE FOUND A RATHER NICE NATURAL SWIMMING POOL.
GREAT NEWS!
MARK, LET'S GIVE OURSELVES AN HOUR'S REST AND THEN WE'LL GET STARTED ON REPAIRING THE VEHICLE, ALL RIGHT?
PERFECT!
WHAT ARE YOU DOING? DON'T YOU WANT TO COME OUTSIDE? IT'S TOO HOT IN HERE!
I DON'T WANT TO...
LEO
NO, MAI LAN, I'M NOT GOING TO LET YOU STAY HERE ALL DAY LONG, CRYING IN A CORNER. YOU HAVE TO PULL YOURSELF TOGETHER!
I CAN'T STOP THINKING ABOUT IT! I HAD HER IN MY ARMS AND SHE ... SHE...
8

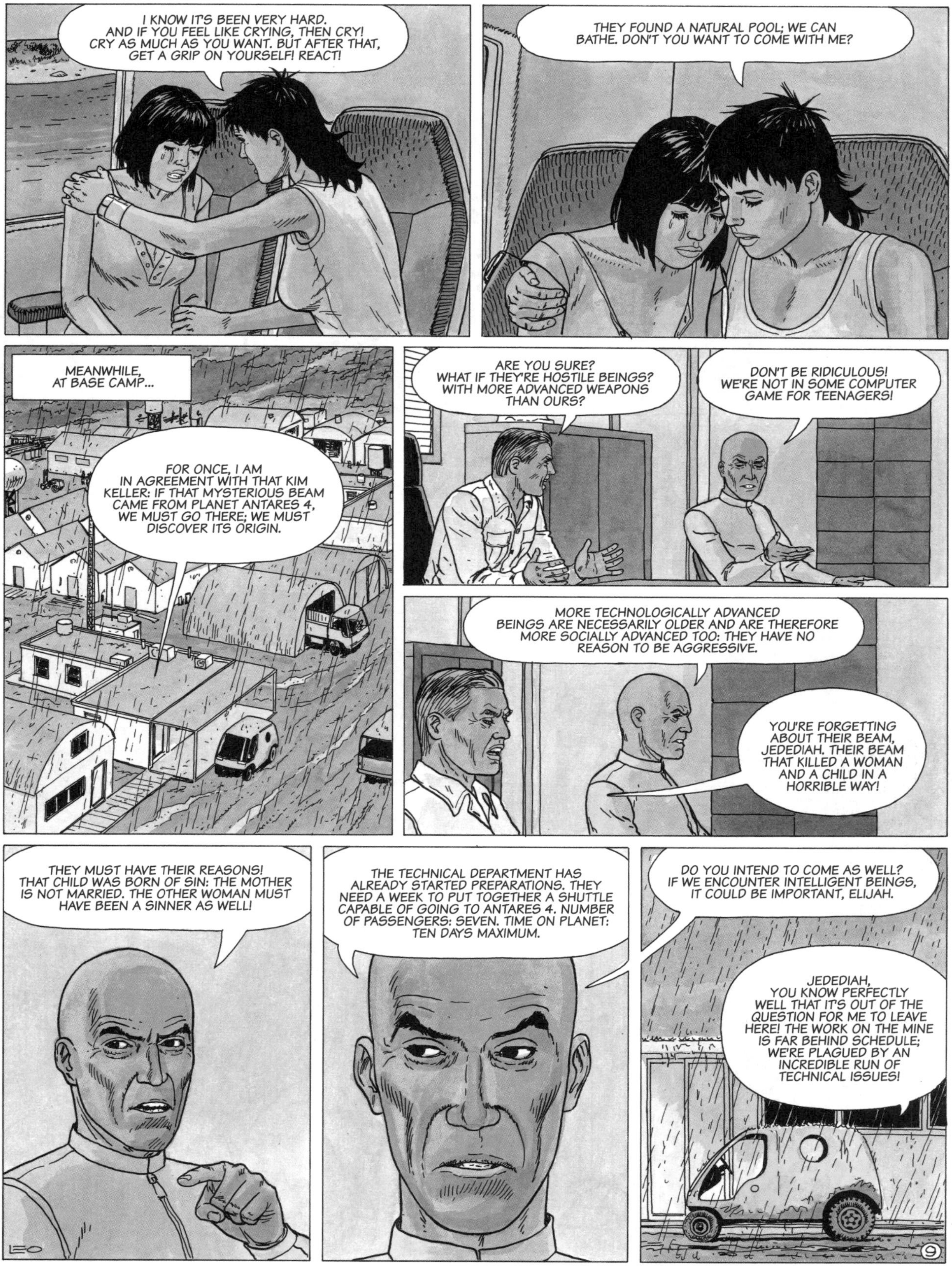
I KNOW IT'S BEEN VERY HARD. AND IF YOU FEEL LIKE CRYING, THEN CRY! CRY AS MUCH AS YOU WANT. BUT AFTER THAT, GET A GRIP ON YOURSELF! REACT!
THEY FOUND A NATURAL POOL; WE CAN BATHE. DON'T YOU WANT TO COME WITH ME?
MEANWHILE, AT BASE CAMP...
FOR ONCE, I AM IN AGREEMENT WITH THAT KIM KELLER: IF THAT MYSTERIOUS BEAM CAME FROM PLANET ANTARES 4, WE MUST GO THERE; WE MUST DISCOVER ITS ORIGIN.
ARE YOU SURE? WHAT IF THEY'RE HOSTILE BEINGS? WITH MORE ADVANCED WEAPONS THAN OURS?
DON'T BE RIDICULOUS! WE'RE NOT IN SOME COMPUTER GAME FOR TEENAGERS!
MORE TECHNOLOGICALLY ADVANCED BEINGS ARE NECESSARILY OLDER AND ARE THEREFORE MORE SOCIALLY ADVANCED TOO: THEY HAVE NO REASON TO BE AGGRESSIVE.
YOU'RE FORGETTING ABOUT THEIR BEAM, JEDEDIAH. THEIR BEAM THAT KILLED A WOMAN AND A CHILD IN A HORRIBLE WAY!
THEY MUST HAVE THEIR REASONS! THAT CHILD WAS BORN OF SIN: THE MOTHER IS NOT MARRIED. THE OTHER WOMAN MUST HAVE BEEN A SINNER AS WELL!
THE TECHNICAL DEPARTMENT HAS ALREADY STARTED PREPARATIONS. THEY NEED A WEEK TO PUT TOGETHER A SHUTTLE CAPABLE OF GOING TO ANTARES 4. NUMBER OF PASSENGERS: SEVEN. TIME ON PLANET: TEN DAYS MAXIMUM.
DO YOU INTEND TO COME AS WELL? IF WE ENCOUNTER INTELLIGENT BEINGS, IT COULD BE IMPORTANT, ELIJAH.
JEDEDIAH, YOU KNOW PERFECTLY WELL THAT IT'S OUT OF THE QUESTION FOR ME TO LEAVE HERE! THE WORK ON THE MINE IS FAR BEHIND SCHEDULE; WE'RE PLAGUED BY AN INCREDIBLE RUN OF TECHNICAL ISSUES!
LEO
9

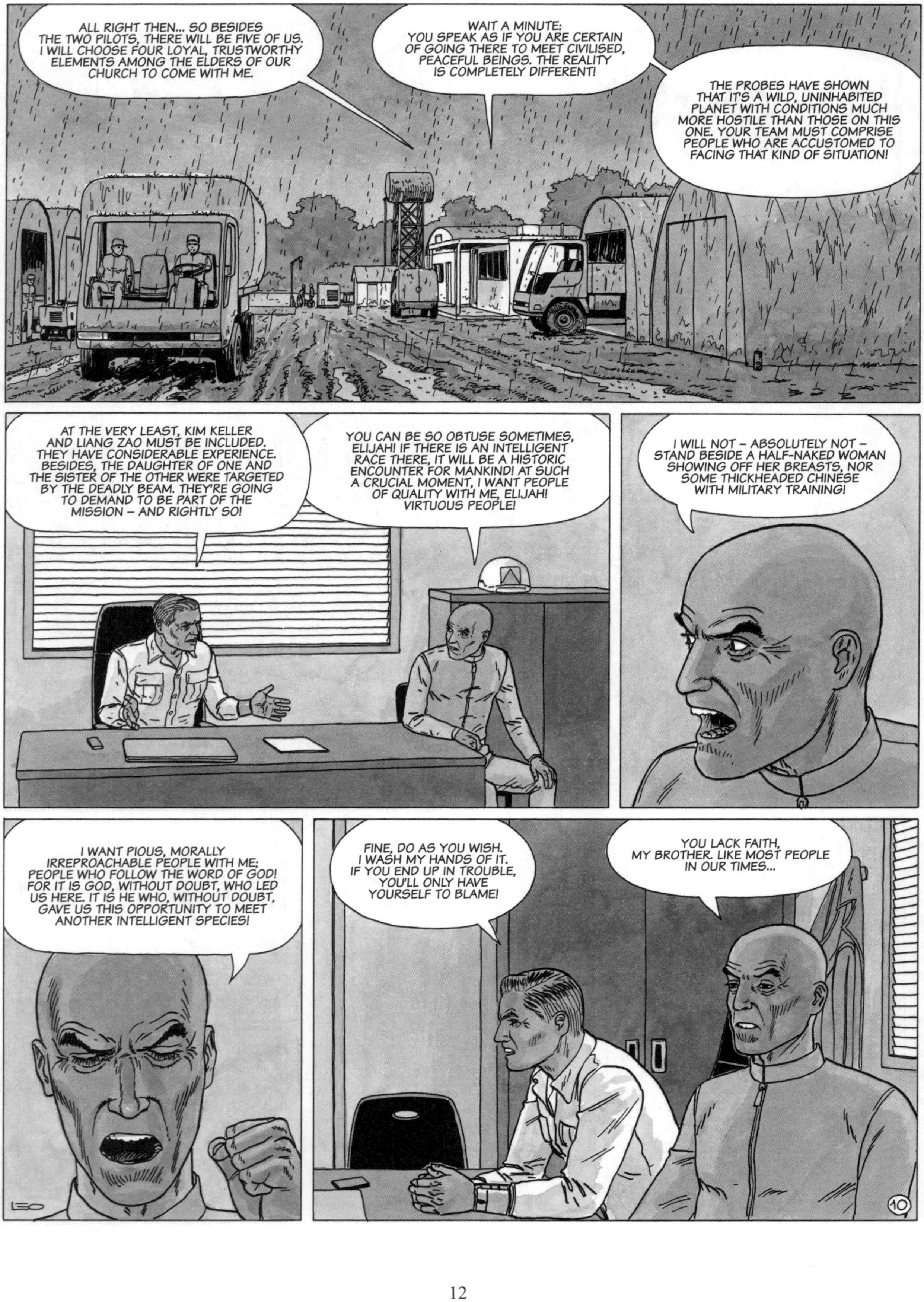
ALL RIGHT THEN... SO BESIDES THE TWO PILOTS, THERE WILL BE FIVE OF US. I WILL CHOOSE FOUR LOYAL, TRUSTWORTHY ELEMENTS AMONG THE ELDERS OF OUR CHURCH TO COME WITH ME.
WAIT A MINUTE: YOU SPEAK AS IF YOU ARE CERTAIN OF GOING THERE TO MEET CIVILISED, PEACEFUL BEINGS. THE REALITY IS COMPLETELY DIFFERENT!
THE PROBES HAVE SHOWN THAT IT'S A WILD, UNINHABITED PLANET WITH CONDITIONS MUCH MORE HOSTILE THAN THOSE ON THIS ONE. YOUR TEAM MUST COMPRISE PEOPLE WHO ARE ACCUSTOMED TO FACING THAT KIND OF SITUATION!
AT THE VERY LEAST, KIM KELLER AND LIANG ZAO MUST BE INCLUDED. THEY HAVE CONSIDERABLE EXPERIENCE. BESIDES, THE DAUGHTER OF ONE AND THE SISTER OF THE OTHER WERE TARGETED BY THE DEADLY BEAM. THEY'RE GOING TO DEMAND TO BE PART OF THE MISSION – AND RIGHTLY SO!
YOU CAN BE SO OBTUSE SOMETIMES, ELIJAH! IF THERE IS AN INTELLIGENT RACE THERE, IT WILL BE A HISTORIC ENCOUNTER FOR MANKIND! AT SUCH A CRUCIAL MOMENT, I WANT PEOPLE OF QUALITY WITH ME, ELIJAH! VIRTUOUS PEOPLE!
I WILL NOT – ABSOLUTELY NOT – STAND BESIDE A HALF-NAKED WOMAN SHOWING OFF HER BREASTS, NOR SOME THICKHEADED CHINESE WITH MILITARY TRAINING!
I WANT PIOUS, MORALLY IRREPROACHABLE PEOPLE WITH ME; PEOPLE WHO FOLLOW THE WORD OF GOD! FOR IT IS GOD, WITHOUT DOUBT, WHO LED US HERE. IT IS HE WHO, WITHOUT DOUBT, GAVE US THIS OPPORTUNITY TO MEET ANOTHER INTELLIGENT SPECIES!
FINE, DO AS YOU WISH. I WASH MY HANDS OF IT. IF YOU END UP IN TROUBLE, YOU'LL ONLY HAVE YOURSELF TO BLAME!
YOU LACK FAITH, MY BROTHER. LIKE MOST PEOPLE IN OUR TIMES...
LEO
10

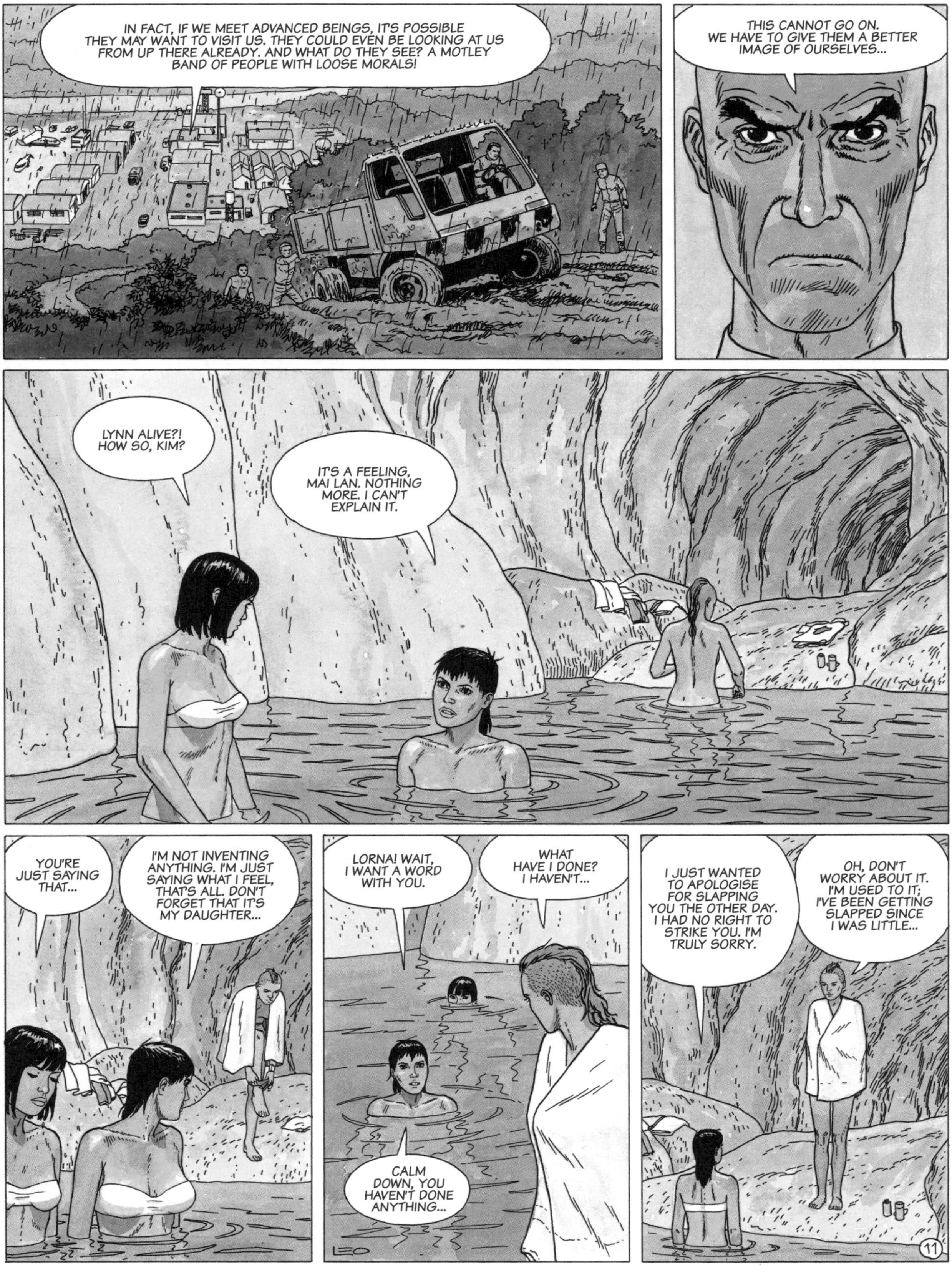
IN FACT, IF WE MEET ADVANCED BEINGS, IT'S POSSIBLE THEY MAY WANT TO VISIT US. THEY COULD EVEN BE LOOKING AT US FROM UP THERE ALREADY. AND WHAT DO THEY SEE? A MOTLEY BAND OF PEOPLE WITH LOOSE MORALS!
THIS CANNOT GO ON. WE HAVE TO GIVE THEM A BETTER IMAGE OF OURSELVES...
LYNN ALIVE?! HOW SO, KIM?
IT'S A FEELING, MAI LAN. NOTHING MORE. I CAN'T EXPLAIN IT.
YOU'RE JUST SAYING THAT...
I'M NOT INVENTING ANYTHING. I'M JUST SAYING WHAT I FEEL, THAT'S ALL. DON'T FORGET THAT IT'S MY DAUGHTER...
LORNA! WAIT, I WANT A WORD WITH YOU.
WHAT HAVE I DONE? I HAVEN'T...
CALM DOWN, YOU HAVEN'T DONE ANYTHING...
I JUST WANTED TO APOLOGISE FOR SLAPPING YOU THE OTHER DAY. I HAD NO RIGHT TO STRIKE YOU. I'M TRULY SORRY.
OH, DON'T WORRY ABOUT IT. I'M USED TO IT; I'VE BEEN GETTING SLAPPED SINCE I WAS LITTLE...
LEO
11

WHY DO YOU DO ALL THIS, LORNA? WHAT ARE YOU TRYING TO ACHIEVE?

WHY DO I DO WHAT?

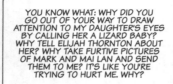

YOU KNOW WHAT: WHY DID YOU GO OUT OF YOUR WAY TO DRAW ATTENTION TO MY DAUGHTER'S EYES BY CALLING HER A LIZARD BABY? WHY TELL ELIJAH THORNTON ABOUT HER? WHY TAKE FURTIVE PICTURES OF MARK AND MAI LAN AND SEND THEM TO ME? IT'S LIKE YOU'RE TRYING TO HURT ME. WHY?

THAT GIRL'S A MYSTERY TO ME!

SHE DOES ALL THAT SO YOU'LL NOTICE HER, KIM...

WHAT DO YOU MEAN?

SHE PROBABLY HAS A CRUSH ON YOU. HAVEN'T YOU NOTICED?

WHAT DO YOU MEAN, A CRUSH ON ME? WHERE DID YOU GET THAT IDEA, MAI LAN?!

I CAUGHT HER LOOKING AT YOU WITH PUPPY EYES A FEW TIMES. I'M TELLING YOU, KIM, SHE HAS A CRUSH ON YOU.

BUT THAT'S RIDICULOUS – SHE'S A KID! SHE'S YOUNG ENOUGH TO BE MY DAUGHTER!... WELL, MAYBE NOT, BUT ANYWAY I PREFER MEN.

SPEAK TO HER, KIM. SHE SEEMS MUCH TOO BITTER FOR HER AGE.

RIGHT NOW, MAI LAN, THE ONE WHO NEEDS HELP IS ME. I DON'T REALLY HAVE THE STRENGTH TO HELP ANYONE...

14

CAN I ASK YOU A QUESTION, AMOS?

YES?

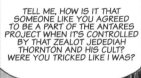

TELL ME, HOW IS IT THAT SOMEONE LIKE YOU AGREED TO BE A PART OF THE ANTARES PROJECT WHEN IT'S CONTROLLED BY THAT ZEALOT JEDEDIAH THORNTON AND HIS CULT? WERE YOU TRICKED LIKE I WAS?

ER... YES! THE THING IS I WAS GOING THROUGH A DIFFICULT PERIOD OF MY LIFE AND I HAD TO LEAVE EARTH AT ALL COSTS – GET A CHANGE OF AIR! IF THE PROJECT'S CONTROLLED BY A CULT OR BY THE POPE HIMSELF – I REALLY COULDN'T HAVE CARED LESS BACK THEN...

STUPID, EH?...

ARE YOU OK, KIM? HOLDING UP?

YES, I'M HOLDING UP.

I HAVE TO BECAUSE THERE'S SOMETHING I MUST DO, AMOS. I MUST GO AND LOOK FOR MY DAUGHTER!...

KIM! DOCTOR! COME AND SEE THIS! IT'S... IT'S INCREDIBLE!

WHAT'S GOING ON?

COME AND SEE! COME AND SEE!

WE WERE EXPLORING THE VARIOUS CAVES AROUND HERE, ALL MORE OR LESS LINKED BY TUNNELS LIKE THIS ONE...

...WHEN WE FOUND THIS.

13

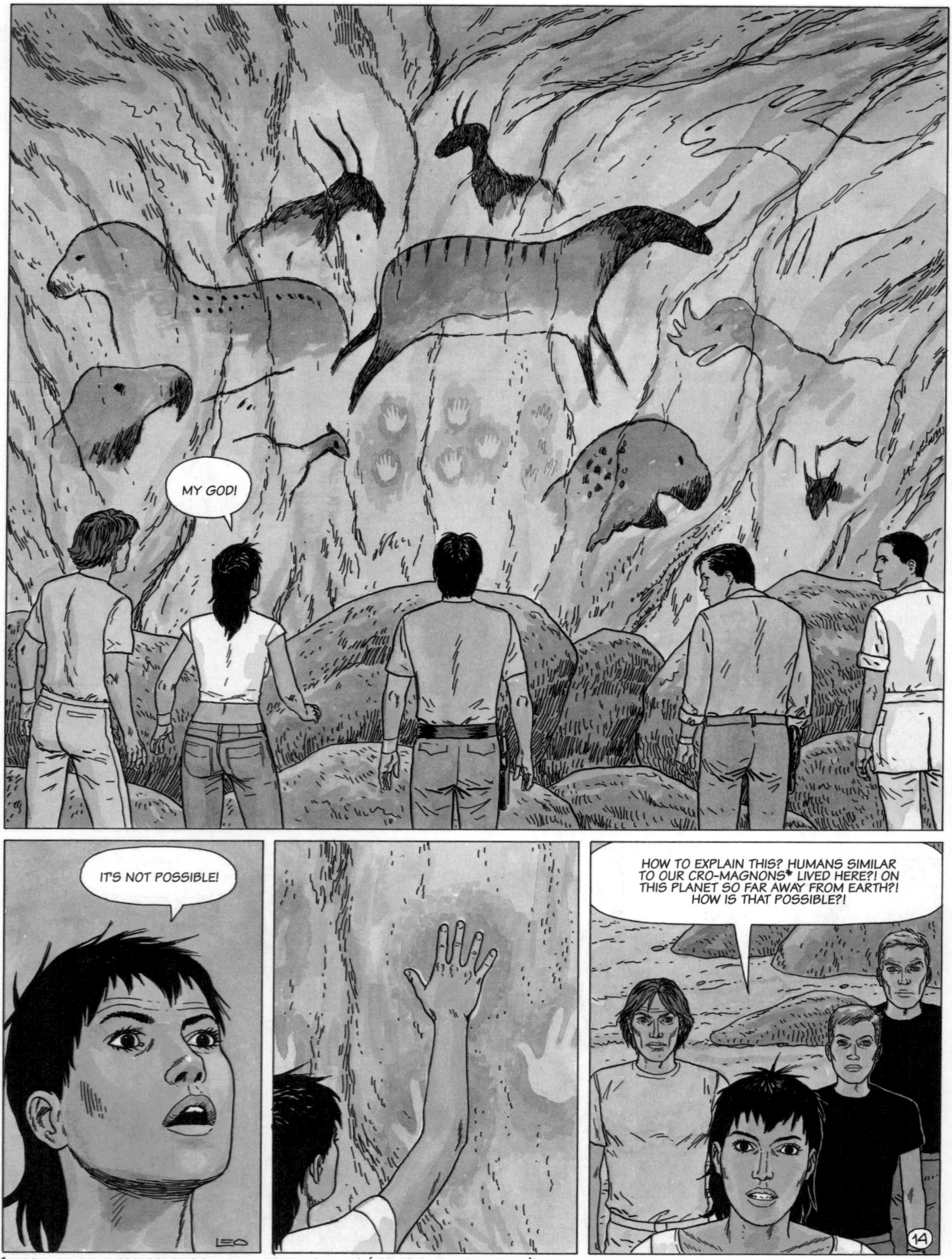
MY GOD!
IT'S NOT POSSIBLE!
HOW TO EXPLAIN THIS? HUMANS SIMILAR TO OUR CRO-MAGNONS* LIVED HERE?! ON THIS PLANET SO FAR AWAY FROM EARTH?! HOW IS THAT POSSIBLE?!
LEO
14

*INFORMAL NAME FOR THE FIRST EARLY MODERN HUMANS (*HOMO SAPIENS SAPIENS*) IN EUROPE AROUND 43,000 YEARS AGO.

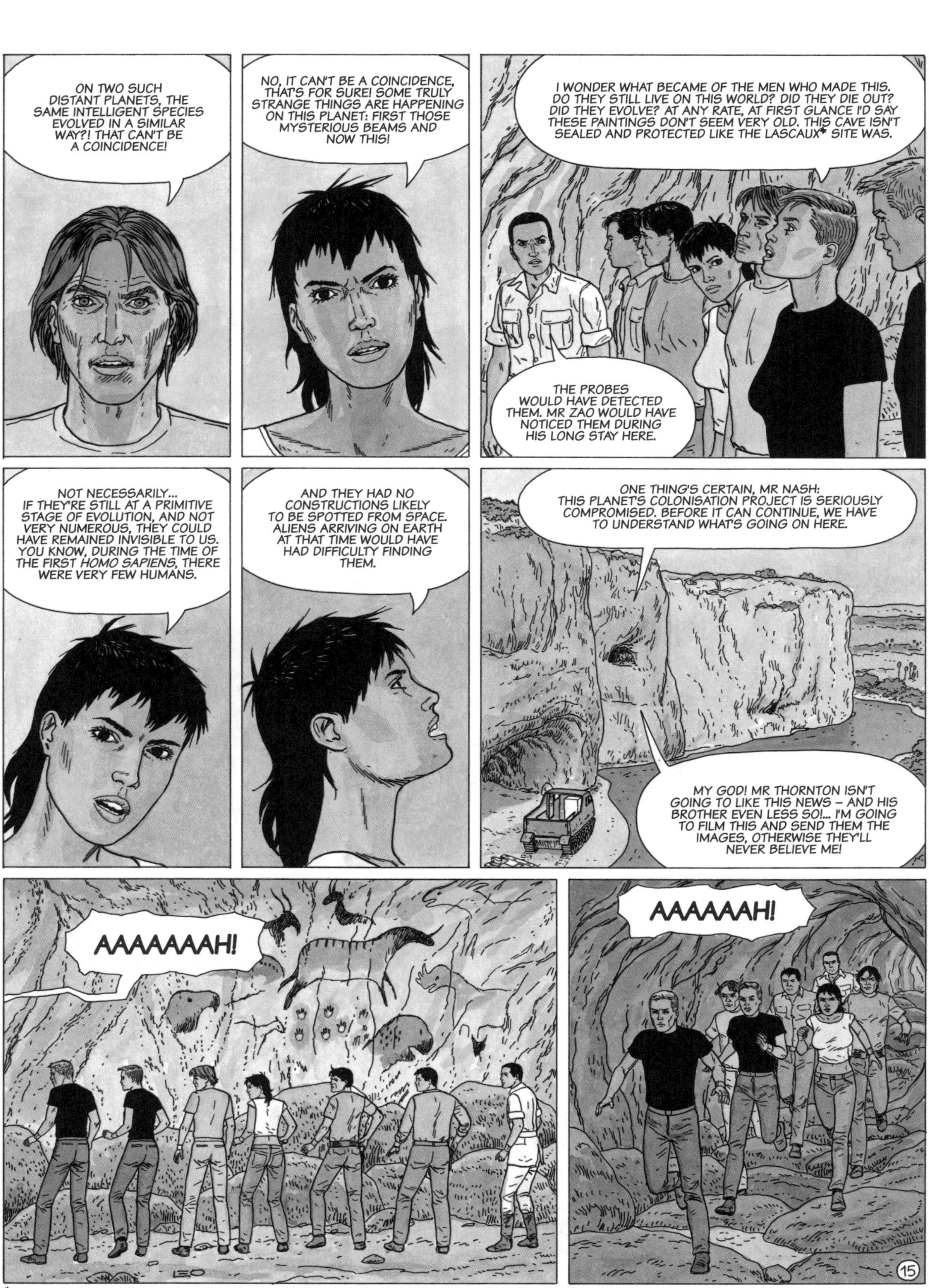
ON TWO SUCH DISTANT PLANETS, THE SAME INTELLIGENT SPECIES EVOLVED IN A SIMILAR WAY?! THAT CAN'T BE A COINCIDENCE!
NO, IT CAN'T BE A COINCIDENCE, THAT'S FOR SURE! SOME TRULY STRANGE THINGS ARE HAPPENING ON THIS PLANET: FIRST THOSE MYSTERIOUS BEAMS AND NOW THIS!
I WONDER WHAT BECAME OF THE MEN WHO MADE THIS. DO THEY STILL LIVE ON THIS WORLD? DID THEY DIE OUT? DID THEY EVOLVE? AT ANY RATE, AT FIRST GLANCE I'D SAY THESE PAINTINGS DON'T SEEM VERY OLD. THIS CAVE ISN'T SEALED AND PROTECTED LIKE THE LASCAUX* SITE WAS.
THE PROBES WOULD HAVE DETECTED THEM. MR ZAO WOULD HAVE NOTICED THEM DURING HIS LONG STAY HERE.
NOT NECESSARILY... IF THEY'RE STILL AT A PRIMITIVE STAGE OF EVOLUTION, AND NOT VERY NUMEROUS, THEY COULD HAVE REMAINED INVISIBLE TO US. YOU KNOW, DURING THE TIME OF THE FIRST *HOMO SAPIENS*, THERE WERE VERY FEW HUMANS.
AND THEY HAD NO CONSTRUCTIONS LIKELY TO BE SPOTTED FROM SPACE. ALIENS ARRIVING ON EARTH AT THAT TIME WOULD HAVE HAD DIFFICULTY FINDING THEM.
ONE THING'S CERTAIN, MR NASH: THIS PLANET'S COLONISATION PROJECT IS SERIOUSLY COMPROMISED. BEFORE IT CAN CONTINUE, WE HAVE TO UNDERSTAND WHAT'S GOING ON HERE.
MY GOD! MR THORNTON ISN'T GOING TO LIKE THIS NEWS – AND HIS BROTHER EVEN LESS SO!... I'M GOING TO FILM THIS AND SEND THEM THE IMAGES, OTHERWISE THEY'LL NEVER BELIEVE ME!
AAAAAAAH!
AAAAAAH!
LEO
15

*A CAVE NETWORK IN SOUTH-WESTERN FRANCE, FAMOUS FOR ITS 17,000-YEAR-OLD PALAEOLITHIC PAINTINGS.

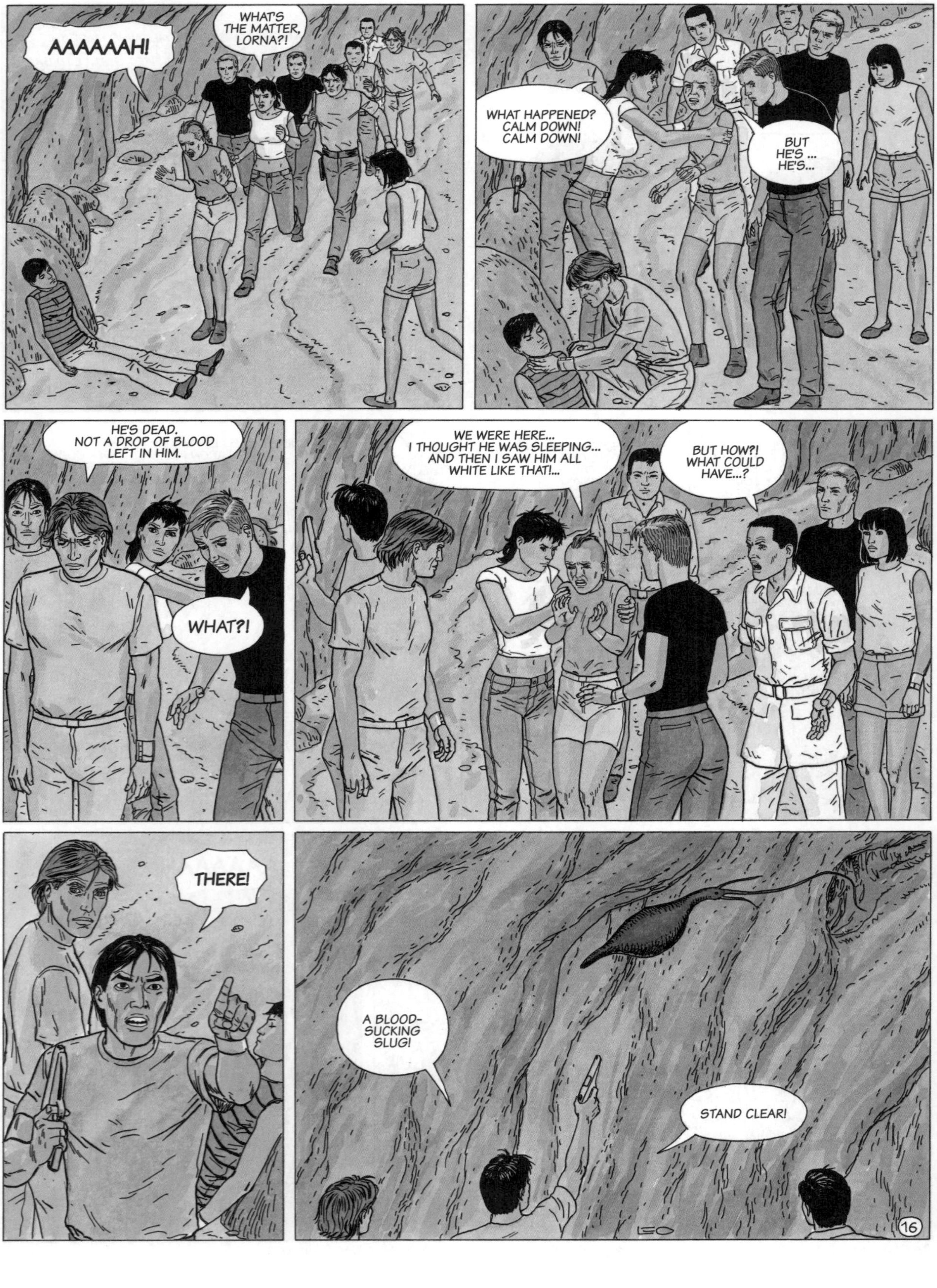
AAAAAAH!
WHAT'S THE MATTER, LORNA?!
WHAT HAPPENED? CALM DOWN! CALM DOWN!
BUT HE'S ... HE'S...
HE'S DEAD. NOT A DROP OF BLOOD LEFT IN HIM.
WHAT?!
WE WERE HERE... I THOUGHT HE WAS SLEEPING... AND THEN I SAW HIM ALL WHITE LIKE THAT!...
BUT HOW?! WHAT COULD HAVE...?
THERE!
A BLOOD-SUCKING SLUG!
STAND CLEAR!
LEO
16

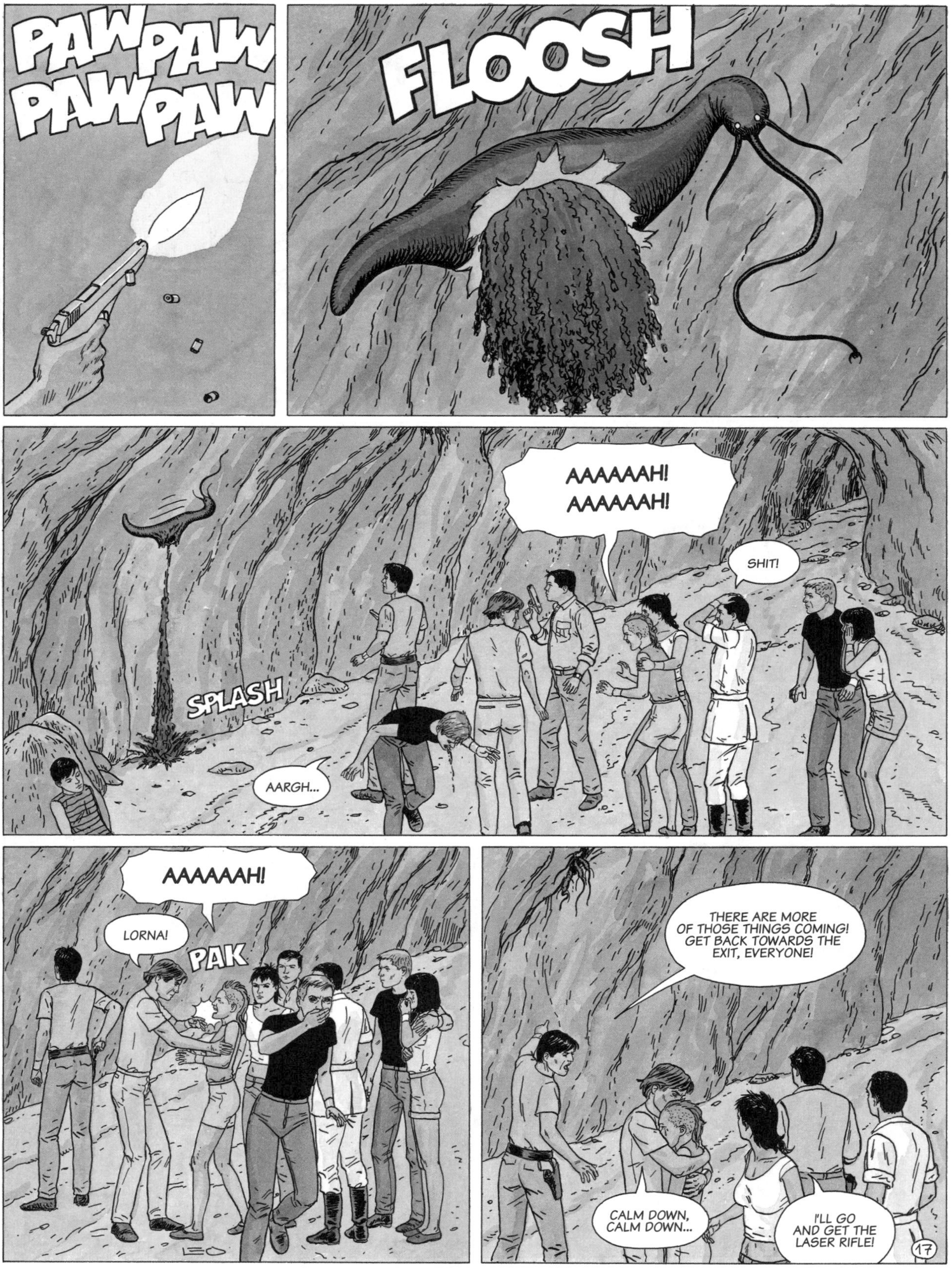
PAW PAW PAW PAW
FLOOSH
AAAAAAH! AAAAAAH!
SHIT!
SPLASH
AARGH...
AAAAAAH!
LORNA!
PAK
THERE ARE MORE OF THOSE THINGS COMING! GET BACK TOWARDS THE EXIT, EVERYONE!
CALM DOWN, CALM DOWN...
I'LL GO AND GET THE LASER RIFLE!
LEO
17

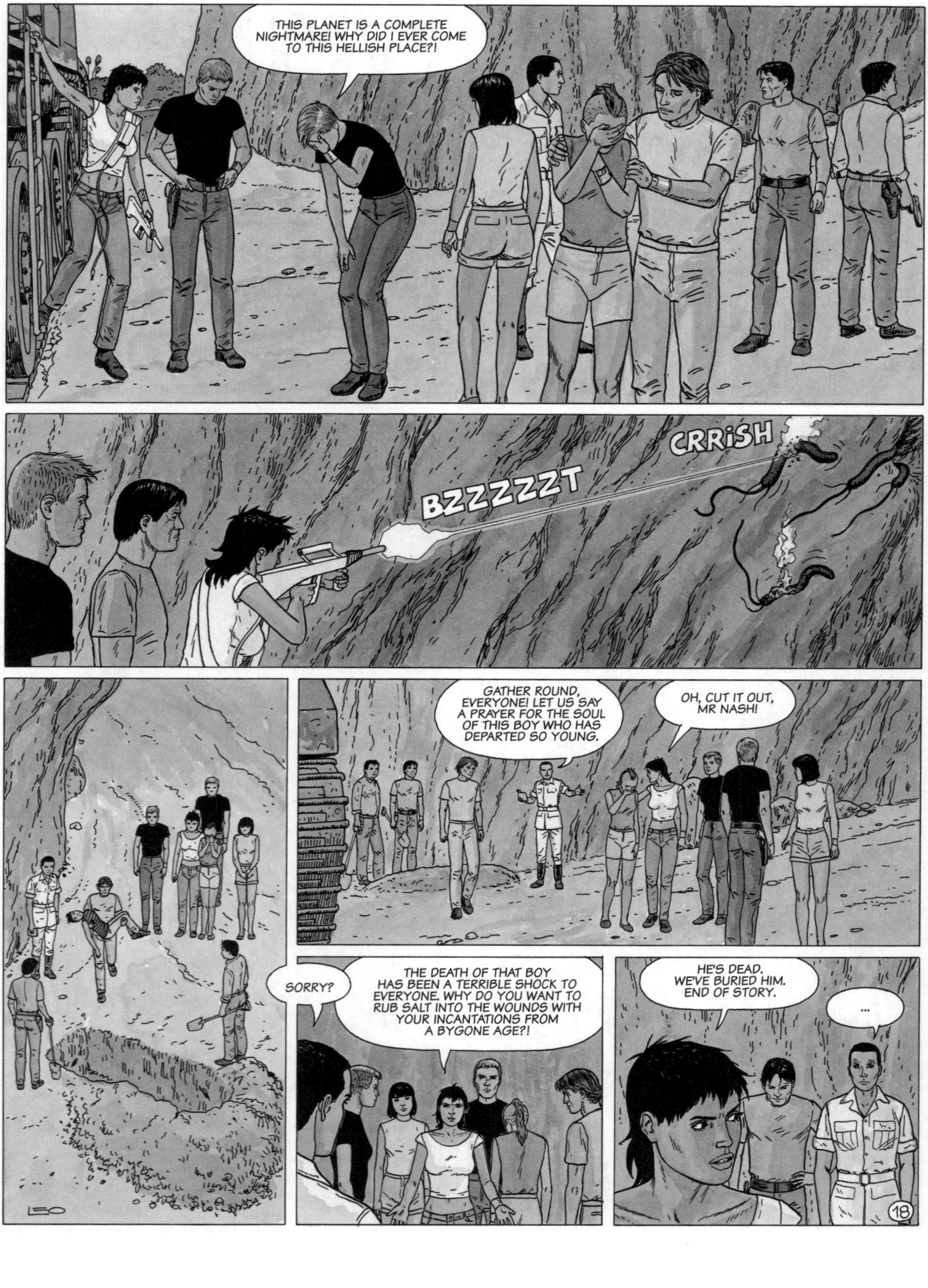
THIS PLANET IS A COMPLETE NIGHTMARE! WHY DID I EVER COME TO THIS HELLISH PLACE?!
BZZZZZT
CRRISH
GATHER ROUND, EVERYONE! LET US SAY A PRAYER FOR THE SOUL OF THIS BOY WHO HAS DEPARTED SO YOUNG.
OH, CUT IT OUT, MR NASH!
SORRY?
THE DEATH OF THAT BOY HAS BEEN A TERRIBLE SHOCK TO EVERYONE. WHY DO YOU WANT TO RUB SALT INTO THE WOUNDS WITH YOUR INCANTATIONS FROM A BYGONE AGE?!
HE'S DEAD. WE'VE BURIED HIM. END OF STORY.
...
LEO
18

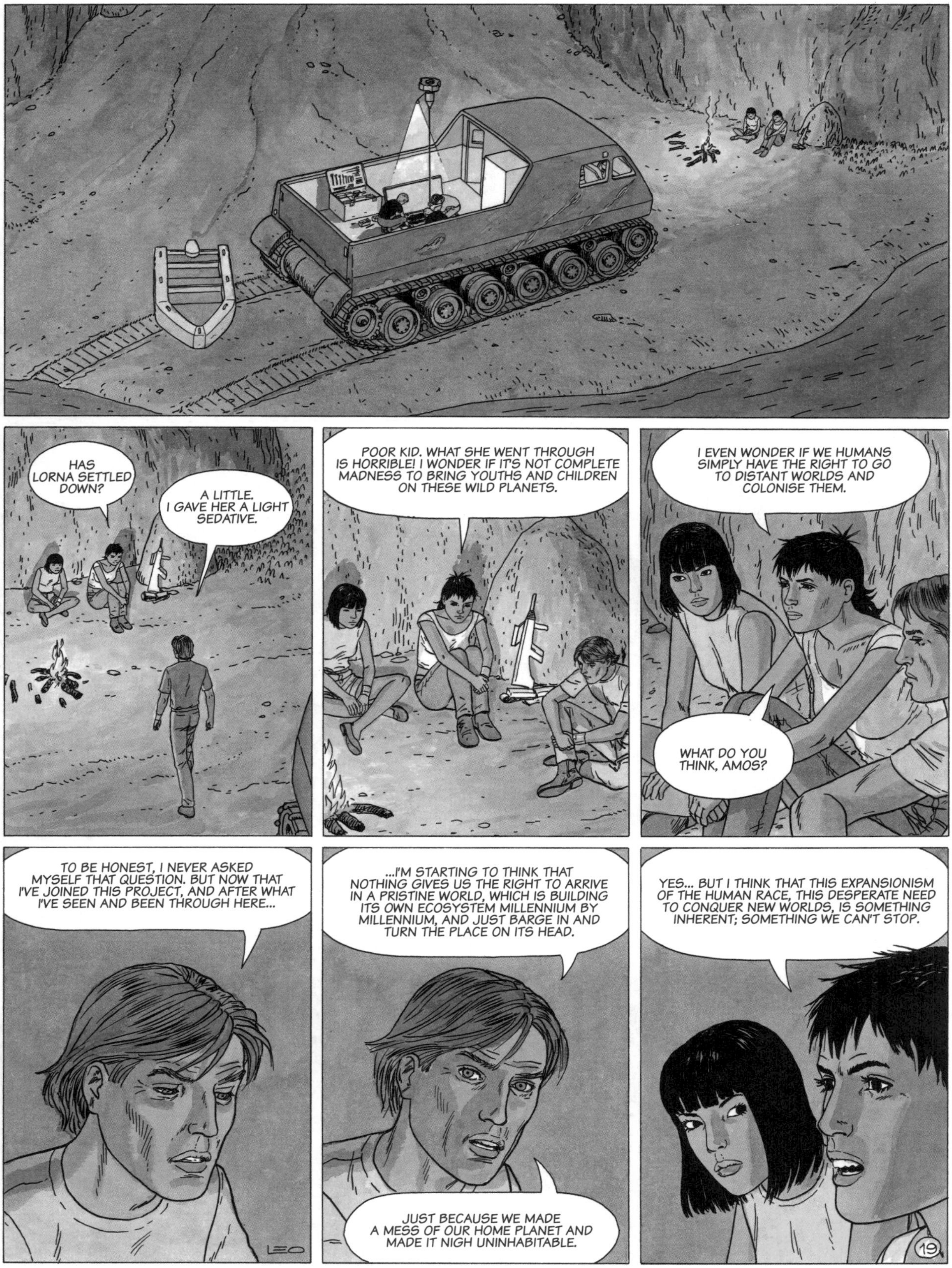
HAS LORNA SETTLED DOWN?
A LITTLE. I GAVE HER A LIGHT SEDATIVE.
POOR KID. WHAT SHE WENT THROUGH IS HORRIBLE! I WONDER IF IT'S NOT COMPLETE MADNESS TO BRING YOUTHS AND CHILDREN ON THESE WILD PLANETS.
I EVEN WONDER IF WE HUMANS SIMPLY HAVE THE RIGHT TO GO TO DISTANT WORLDS AND COLONISE THEM.
WHAT DO YOU THINK, AMOS?
TO BE HONEST, I NEVER ASKED MYSELF THAT QUESTION. BUT NOW THAT I'VE JOINED THIS PROJECT, AND AFTER WHAT I'VE SEEN AND BEEN THROUGH HERE...
LEO
...I'M STARTING TO THINK THAT NOTHING GIVES US THE RIGHT TO ARRIVE IN A PRISTINE WORLD, WHICH IS BUILDING ITS OWN ECOSYSTEM MILLENNIUM BY MILLENNIUM, AND JUST BARGE IN AND TURN THE PLACE ON ITS HEAD.
JUST BECAUSE WE MADE A MESS OF OUR HOME PLANET AND MADE IT NIGH UNINHABITABLE.
YES... BUT I THINK THAT THIS EXPANSIONISM OF THE HUMAN RACE, THIS DESPERATE NEED TO CONQUER NEW WORLDS, IS SOMETHING INHERENT; SOMETHING WE CAN'T STOP.
19

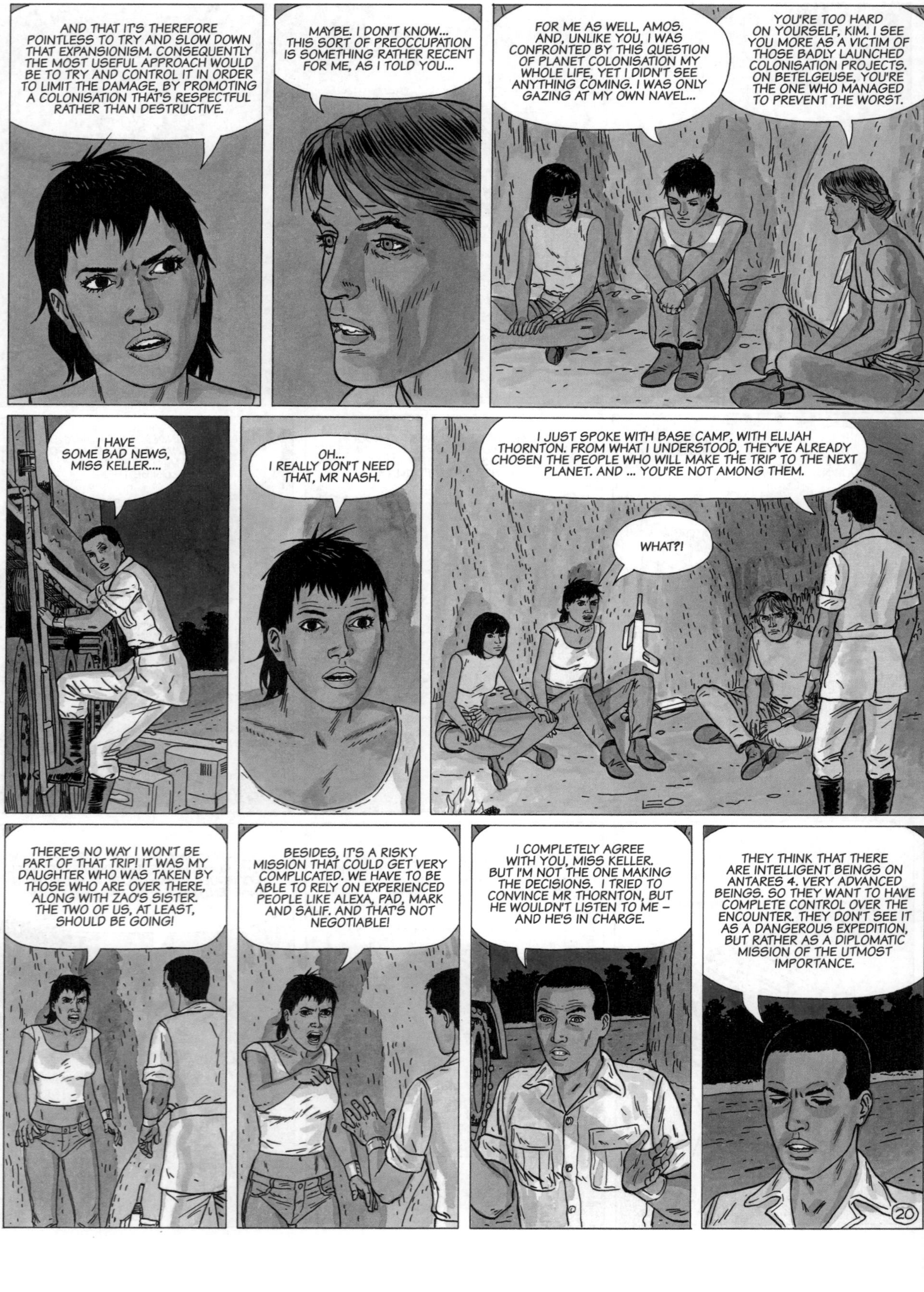
AND THAT IT'S THEREFORE POINTLESS TO TRY AND SLOW DOWN THAT EXPANSIONISM. CONSEQUENTLY THE MOST USEFUL APPROACH WOULD BE TO TRY AND CONTROL IT IN ORDER TO LIMIT THE DAMAGE, BY PROMOTING A COLONISATION THAT'S RESPECTFUL RATHER THAN DESTRUCTIVE.
MAYBE. I DON'T KNOW... THIS SORT OF PREOCCUPATION IS SOMETHING RATHER RECENT FOR ME, AS I TOLD YOU...
FOR ME AS WELL, AMOS. AND, UNLIKE YOU, I WAS CONFRONTED BY THIS QUESTION OF PLANET COLONISATION MY WHOLE LIFE, YET I DIDN'T SEE ANYTHING COMING. I WAS ONLY GAZING AT MY OWN NAVEL...
YOU'RE TOO HARD ON YOURSELF, KIM. I SEE YOU MORE AS A VICTIM OF THOSE BADLY LAUNCHED COLONISATION PROJECTS. ON BETELGEUSE, YOU'RE THE ONE WHO MANAGED TO PREVENT THE WORST.
I HAVE SOME BAD NEWS, MISS KELLER....
OH... I REALLY DON'T NEED THAT, MR NASH.
I JUST SPOKE WITH BASE CAMP, WITH ELIJAH THORNTON. FROM WHAT I UNDERSTOOD, THEY'VE ALREADY CHOSEN THE PEOPLE WHO WILL MAKE THE TRIP TO THE NEXT PLANET. AND ... YOU'RE NOT AMONG THEM.
WHAT?!
LEO
THERE'S NO WAY I WON'T BE PART OF THAT TRIP! IT WAS MY DAUGHTER WHO WAS TAKEN BY THOSE WHO ARE OVER THERE, ALONG WITH ZAO'S SISTER. THE TWO OF US, AT LEAST, SHOULD BE GOING!
BESIDES, IT'S A RISKY MISSION THAT COULD GET VERY COMPLICATED. WE HAVE TO BE ABLE TO RELY ON EXPERIENCED PEOPLE LIKE ALEXA, PAD, MARK AND SALIF. AND THAT'S NOT NEGOTIABLE!
I COMPLETELY AGREE WITH YOU, MISS KELLER. BUT I'M NOT THE ONE MAKING THE DECISIONS. I TRIED TO CONVINCE MR THORNTON, BUT HE WOULDN'T LISTEN TO ME – AND HE'S IN CHARGE.
THEY THINK THAT THERE ARE INTELLIGENT BEINGS ON ANTARES 4. VERY ADVANCED BEINGS. SO THEY WANT TO HAVE COMPLETE CONTROL OVER THE ENCOUNTER. THEY DON'T SEE IT AS A DANGEROUS EXPEDITION, BUT RATHER AS A DIPLOMATIC MISSION OF THE UTMOST IMPORTANCE.
20

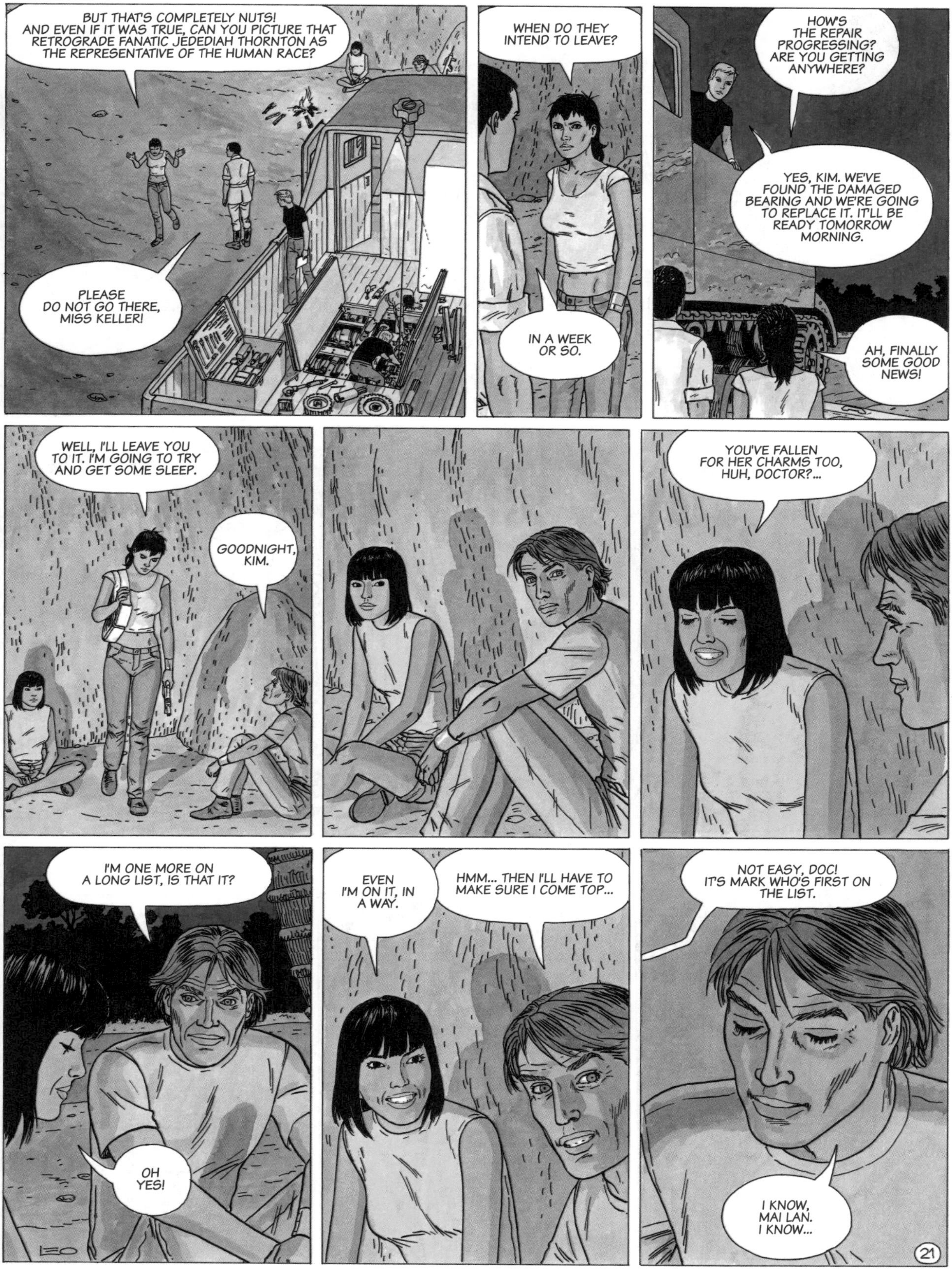
BUT THAT'S COMPLETELY NUTS! AND EVEN IF IT WAS TRUE, CAN YOU PICTURE THAT RETROGRADE FANATIC JEDEDIAH THORNTON AS THE REPRESENTATIVE OF THE HUMAN RACE?
PLEASE DO NOT GO THERE, MISS KELLER!
WHEN DO THEY INTEND TO LEAVE?
IN A WEEK OR SO.
HOW'S THE REPAIR PROGRESSING? ARE YOU GETTING ANYWHERE?
YES, KIM. WE'VE FOUND THE DAMAGED BEARING AND WE'RE GOING TO REPLACE IT. IT'LL BE READY TOMORROW MORNING.
AH, FINALLY SOME GOOD NEWS!
WELL, I'LL LEAVE YOU TO IT. I'M GOING TO TRY AND GET SOME SLEEP.
GOODNIGHT, KIM.
YOU'VE FALLEN FOR HER CHARMS TOO, HUH, DOCTOR?...
I'M ONE MORE ON A LONG LIST, IS THAT IT?
OH YES!
EVEN I'M ON IT, IN A WAY.
HMM... THEN I'LL HAVE TO MAKE SURE I COME TOP...
NOT EASY, DOC! IT'S MARK WHO'S FIRST ON THE LIST.
I KNOW, MAI LAN. I KNOW...
21

CAN YOU NOT SLEEP? DO YOU WANT ME TO ASK THE DOCTOR FOR A...

HE WAS MY BEST FRIEND... MY ONLY FRIEND...

AND NOW HE'S GONE!... I'M THE LONELIEST PERSON IN THE WORLD!

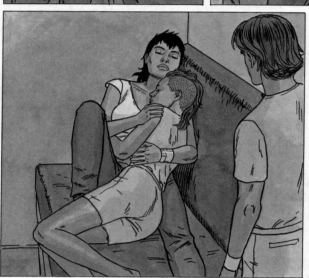

HI! DID YOU SUCCEED?

YES. WE WORKED THROUGH A GOOD PART OF THE NIGHT AND IT'S DONE; WE'VE REPLACED THE BEARING. WE CAN GO.

ZAO? WHAT IS IT?

THE BOAT'S GONE. AND SO HAS MY BROTHER...

22

24

MAYBE HE JUST WENT FISHING OR...

NO. HE LEFT. I KNOW HIM.

BUT HOW IS HE GOING TO MANAGE?! WE'RE STILL A LONG WAY FROM BASE CAMP. HE WON'T BE ABLE TO SURVIVE ALONE!

I KNOW, MARK, I KNOW...

WE COULD STAY HERE FOR A LITTLE WHILE – SEE IF HE COMES BACK.

NO! WE HAVE TO REACH BASE AS SOON AS POSSIBLE SO WE CAN TRY AND CONVINCE THEM TO LET US BE ON THE TRIP TO THE OTHER PLANET. WE HAVE NO TIME TO WASTE. LET'S GO!

MEANWHILE, AT BASE CAMP...

CLACK PLECK

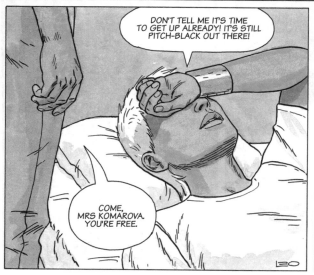

DON'T TELL ME IT'S TIME TO GET UP ALREADY! IT'S STILL PITCH-BLACK OUT THERE!

COME, MRS KOMAROVA. YOU'RE FREE.

WHAT DO YOU MEAN, FREE? WHO ARE YOU?

DON'T YOU REMEMBER? I WAS A POLICE OFFICER. I WAS AMONG THOSE WHO ARRESTED YOU A FEW DAYS AGO.

23

25

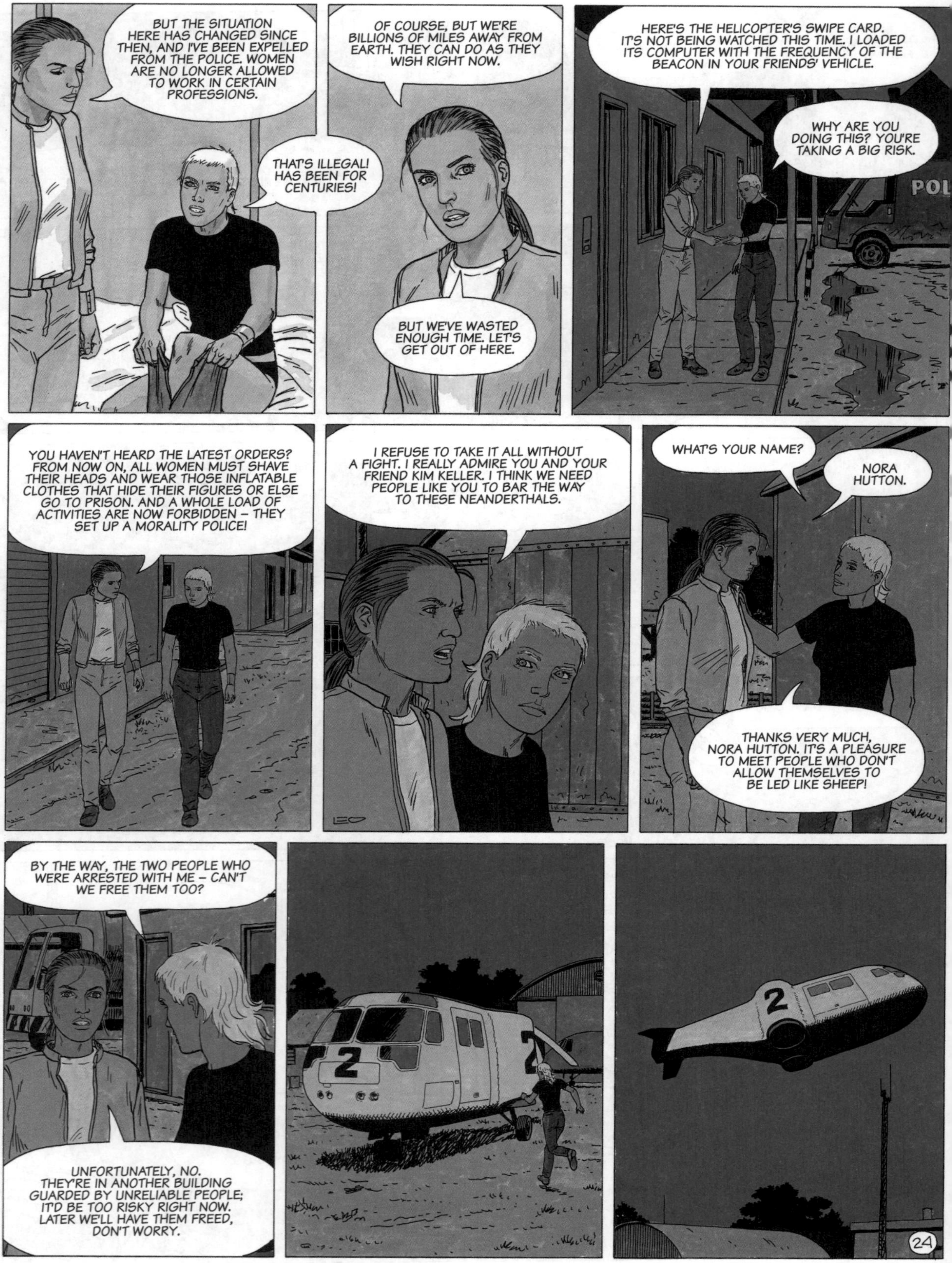
BUT THE SITUATION HERE HAS CHANGED SINCE THEN, AND I'VE BEEN EXPELLED FROM THE POLICE. WOMEN ARE NO LONGER ALLOWED TO WORK IN CERTAIN PROFESSIONS.
THAT'S ILLEGAL! HAS BEEN FOR CENTURIES!
OF COURSE, BUT WE'RE BILLIONS OF MILES AWAY FROM EARTH. THEY CAN DO AS THEY WISH RIGHT NOW.
BUT WE'VE WASTED ENOUGH TIME. LET'S GET OUT OF HERE.
HERE'S THE HELICOPTER'S SWIPE CARD. IT'S NOT BEING WATCHED THIS TIME. I LOADED ITS COMPUTER WITH THE FREQUENCY OF THE BEACON IN YOUR FRIENDS' VEHICLE.
WHY ARE YOU DOING THIS? YOU'RE TAKING A BIG RISK.
POL
YOU HAVEN'T HEARD THE LATEST ORDERS? FROM NOW ON, ALL WOMEN MUST SHAVE THEIR HEADS AND WEAR THOSE INFLATABLE CLOTHES THAT HIDE THEIR FIGURES OR ELSE GO TO PRISON. AND A WHOLE LOAD OF ACTIVITIES ARE NOW FORBIDDEN – THEY SET UP A MORALITY POLICE!
I REFUSE TO TAKE IT ALL WITHOUT A FIGHT. I REALLY ADMIRE YOU AND YOUR FRIEND KIM KELLER. I THINK WE NEED PEOPLE LIKE YOU TO BAR THE WAY TO THESE NEANDERTHALS.
LEO
WHAT'S YOUR NAME?
NORA HUTTON.
THANKS VERY MUCH, NORA HUTTON. IT'S A PLEASURE TO MEET PEOPLE WHO DON'T ALLOW THEMSELVES TO BE LED LIKE SHEEP!
BY THE WAY, THE TWO PEOPLE WHO WERE ARRESTED WITH ME – CAN'T WE FREE THEM TOO?
UNFORTUNATELY, NO. THEY'RE IN ANOTHER BUILDING GUARDED BY UNRELIABLE PEOPLE; IT'D BE TOO RISKY RIGHT NOW. LATER WE'LL HAVE THEM FREED, DON'T WORRY.
2
2
2
24

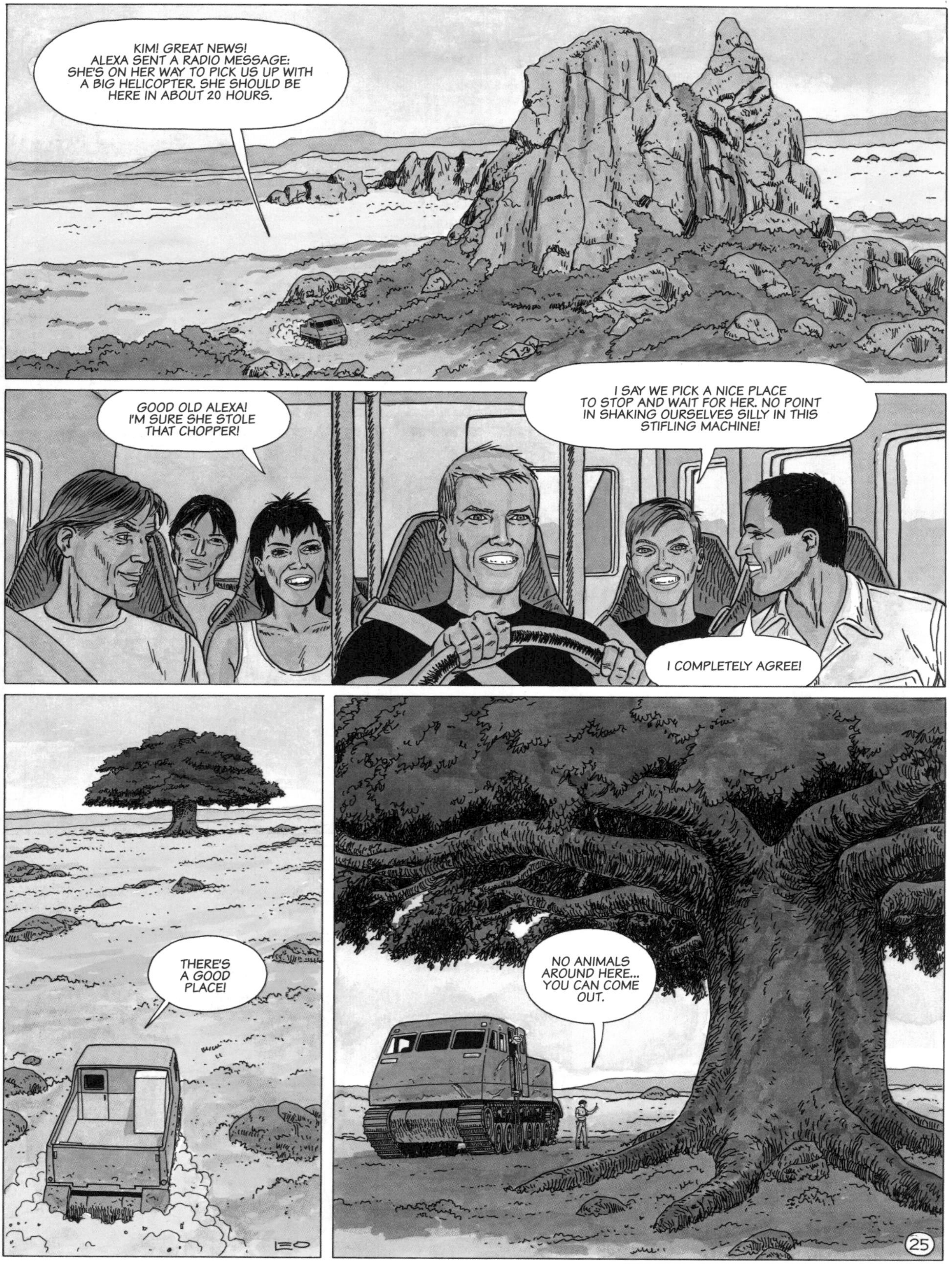
KIM! GREAT NEWS! ALEXA SENT A RADIO MESSAGE: SHE'S ON HER WAY TO PICK US UP WITH A BIG HELICOPTER. SHE SHOULD BE HERE IN ABOUT 20 HOURS.
GOOD OLD ALEXA! I'M SURE SHE STOLE THAT CHOPPER!
I SAY WE PICK A NICE PLACE TO STOP AND WAIT FOR HER. NO POINT IN SHAKING OURSELVES SILLY IN THIS STIFLING MACHINE!
I COMPLETELY AGREE!
THERE'S A GOOD PLACE!
LEO
NO ANIMALS AROUND HERE... YOU CAN COME OUT.
25

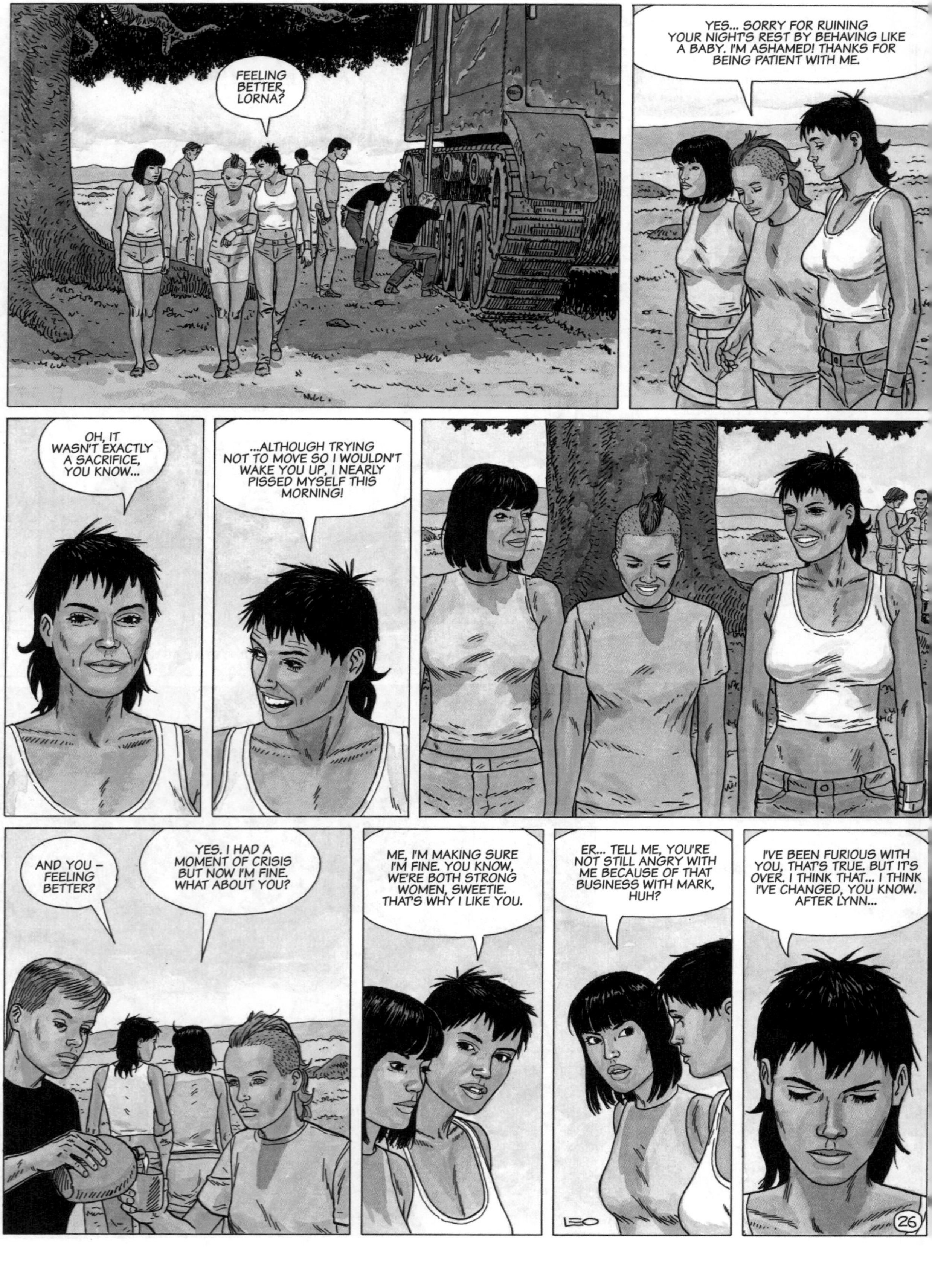
FEELING BETTER, LORNA?
YES... SORRY FOR RUINING YOUR NIGHT'S REST BY BEHAVING LIKE A BABY. I'M ASHAMED! THANKS FOR BEING PATIENT WITH ME.
OH, IT WASN'T EXACTLY A SACRIFICE, YOU KNOW...
...ALTHOUGH TRYING NOT TO MOVE SO I WOULDN'T WAKE YOU UP, I NEARLY PISSED MYSELF THIS MORNING!
AND YOU - FEELING BETTER?
YES. I HAD A MOMENT OF CRISIS BUT NOW I'M FINE. WHAT ABOUT YOU?
ME, I'M MAKING SURE I'M FINE. YOU KNOW, WE'RE BOTH STRONG WOMEN, SWEETIE. THAT'S WHY I LIKE YOU.
ER... TELL ME, YOU'RE NOT STILL ANGRY WITH ME BECAUSE OF THAT BUSINESS WITH MARK, HUH?
I'VE BEEN FURIOUS WITH YOU, THAT'S TRUE. BUT IT'S OVER. I THINK THAT... I THINK I'VE CHANGED, YOU KNOW. AFTER LYNN...
LEO
26

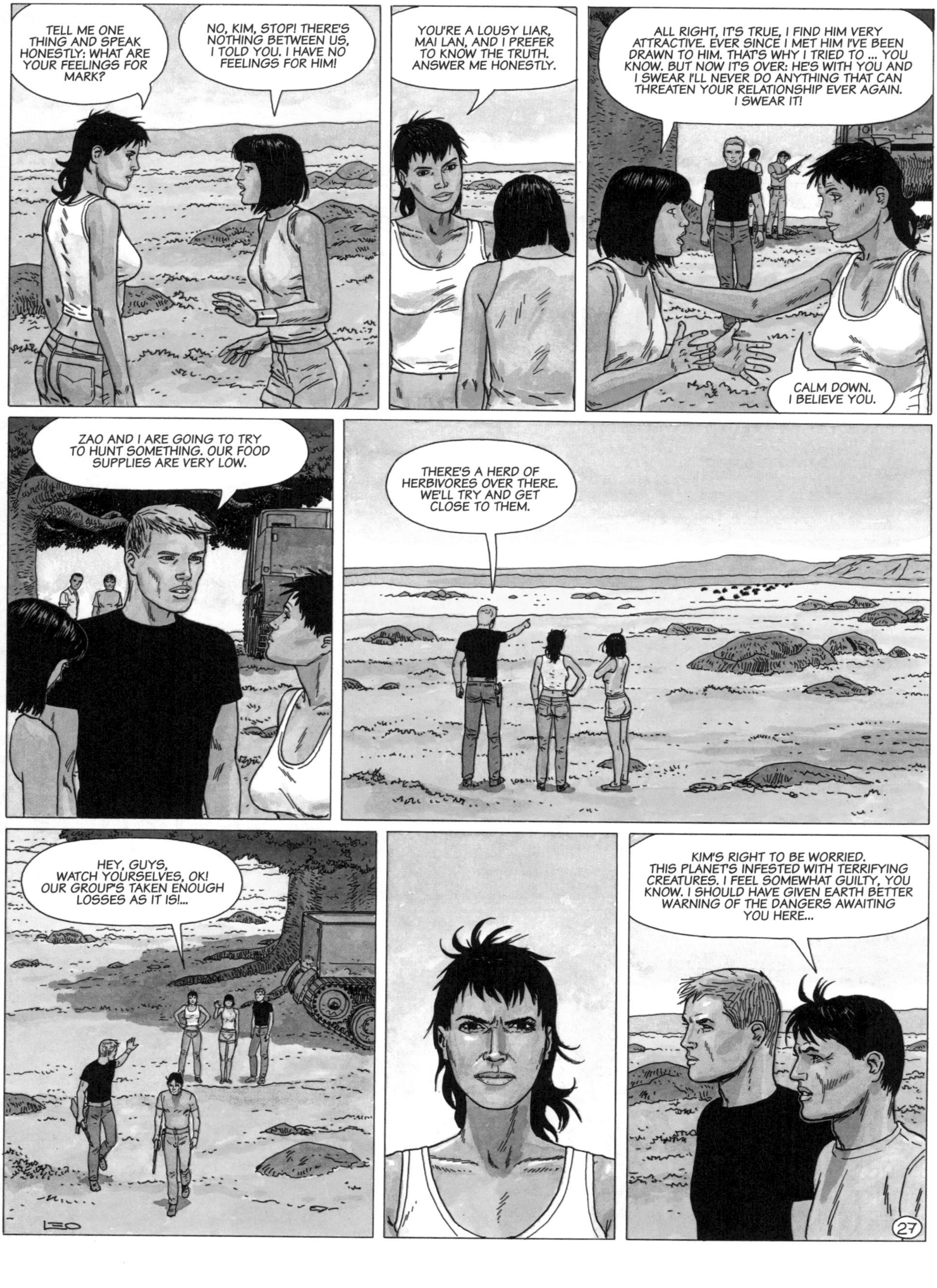
TELL ME ONE THING AND SPEAK HONESTLY: WHAT ARE YOUR FEELINGS FOR MARK?
NO, KIM, STOP! THERE'S NOTHING BETWEEN US, I TOLD YOU. I HAVE NO FEELINGS FOR HIM!
YOU'RE A LOUSY LIAR, MAI LAN, AND I PREFER TO KNOW THE TRUTH. ANSWER ME HONESTLY.
ALL RIGHT, IT'S TRUE, I FIND HIM VERY ATTRACTIVE. EVER SINCE I MET HIM I'VE BEEN DRAWN TO HIM. THAT'S WHY I TRIED TO ... YOU KNOW. BUT NOW IT'S OVER: HE'S WITH YOU AND I SWEAR I'LL NEVER DO ANYTHING THAT CAN THREATEN YOUR RELATIONSHIP EVER AGAIN. I SWEAR IT!
CALM DOWN. I BELIEVE YOU.
ZAO AND I ARE GOING TO TRY TO HUNT SOMETHING. OUR FOOD SUPPLIES ARE VERY LOW.
THERE'S A HERD OF HERBIVORES OVER THERE. WE'LL TRY AND GET CLOSE TO THEM.
HEY, GUYS, WATCH YOURSELVES, OK! OUR GROUP'S TAKEN ENOUGH LOSSES AS IT IS!...
LEO
KIM'S RIGHT TO BE WORRIED. THIS PLANET'S INFESTED WITH TERRIFYING CREATURES. I FEEL SOMEWHAT GUILTY, YOU KNOW. I SHOULD HAVE GIVEN EARTH BETTER WARNING OF THE DANGERS AWAITING YOU HERE...
27

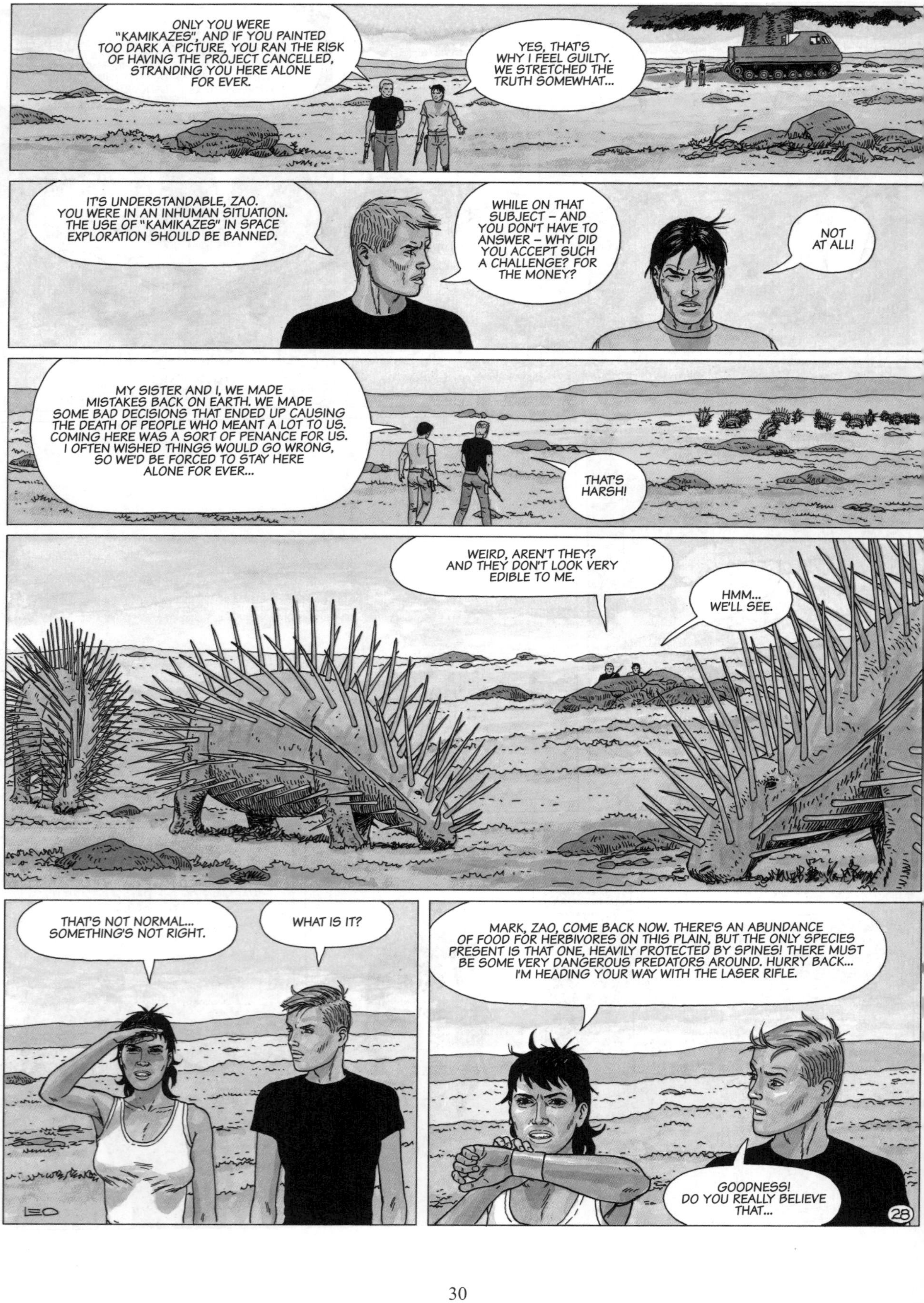
ONLY YOU WERE "KAMIKAZES", AND IF YOU PAINTED TOO DARK A PICTURE, YOU RAN THE RISK OF HAVING THE PROJECT CANCELLED, STRANDING YOU HERE ALONE FOR EVER.
YES, THAT'S WHY I FEEL GUILTY. WE STRETCHED THE TRUTH SOMEWHAT...
IT'S UNDERSTANDABLE, ZAO. YOU WERE IN AN INHUMAN SITUATION. THE USE OF "KAMIKAZES" IN SPACE EXPLORATION SHOULD BE BANNED.
WHILE ON THAT SUBJECT – AND YOU DON'T HAVE TO ANSWER – WHY DID YOU ACCEPT SUCH A CHALLENGE? FOR THE MONEY?
NOT AT ALL!
MY SISTER AND I, WE MADE MISTAKES BACK ON EARTH. WE MADE SOME BAD DECISIONS THAT ENDED UP CAUSING THE DEATH OF PEOPLE WHO MEANT A LOT TO US. COMING HERE WAS A SORT OF PENANCE FOR US. I OFTEN WISHED THINGS WOULD GO WRONG, SO WE'D BE FORCED TO STAY HERE ALONE FOR EVER...
THAT'S HARSH!
WEIRD, AREN'T THEY? AND THEY DON'T LOOK VERY EDIBLE TO ME.
HMM... WE'LL SEE.
THAT'S NOT NORMAL... SOMETHING'S NOT RIGHT.
WHAT IS IT?
MARK, ZAO, COME BACK NOW. THERE'S AN ABUNDANCE OF FOOD FOR HERBIVORES ON THIS PLAIN, BUT THE ONLY SPECIES PRESENT IS THAT ONE, HEAVILY PROTECTED BY SPINES! THERE MUST BE SOME VERY DANGEROUS PREDATORS AROUND. HURRY BACK... I'M HEADING YOUR WAY WITH THE LASER RIFLE.
GOODNESS! DO YOU REALLY BELIEVE THAT...
LEO
28

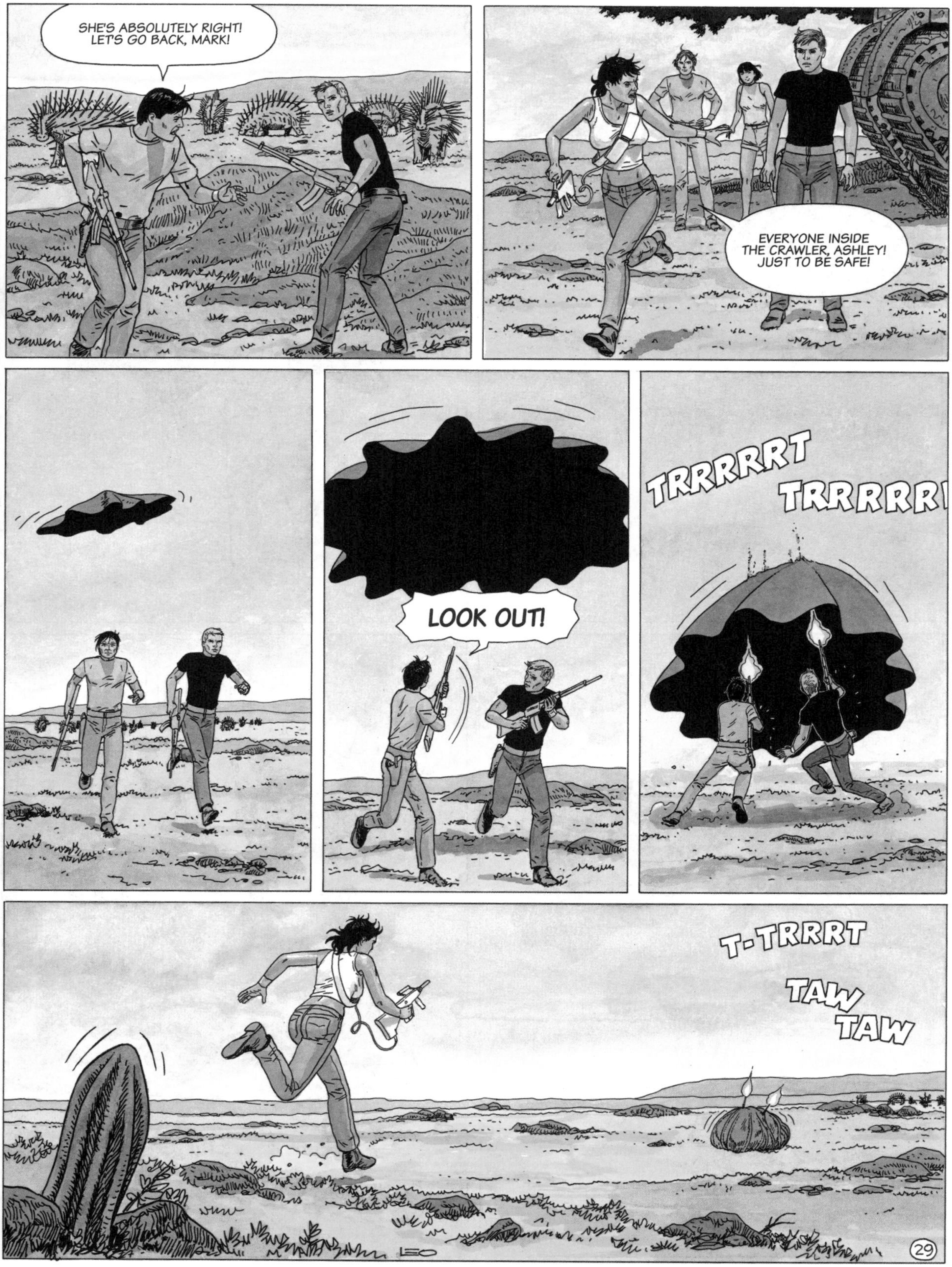
SHE'S ABSOLUTELY RIGHT! LET'S GO BACK, MARK!
EVERYONE INSIDE THE CRAWLER, ASHLEY! JUST TO BE SAFE!
LOOK OUT!
TRRRRRT
TRRRRRT
T-TRRRT
TAW
TAW
LEO
29

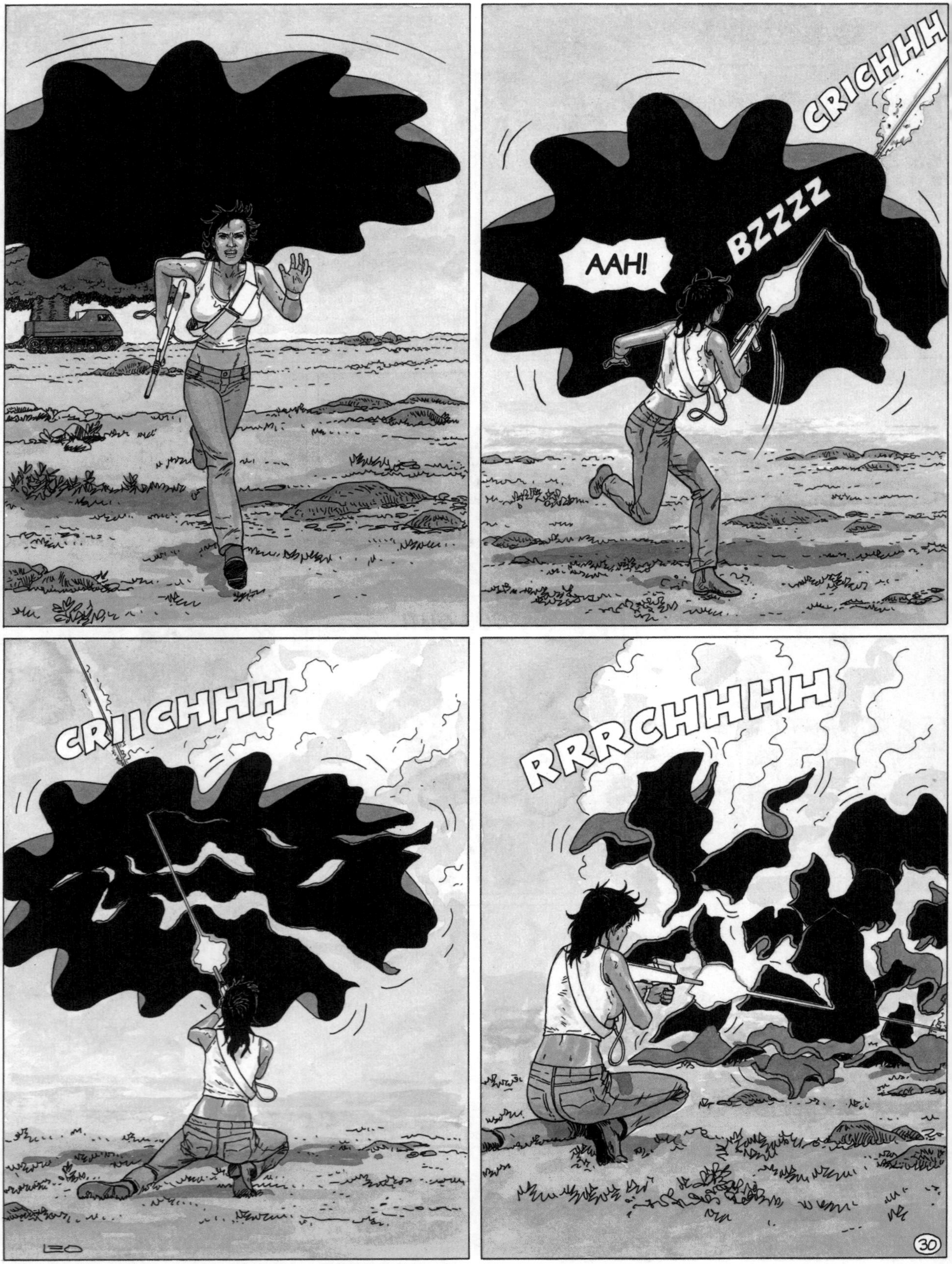
CRICHHH
AAH!
BZZZZ
CRIICHHH
RRRCHHHHH
LEO
30

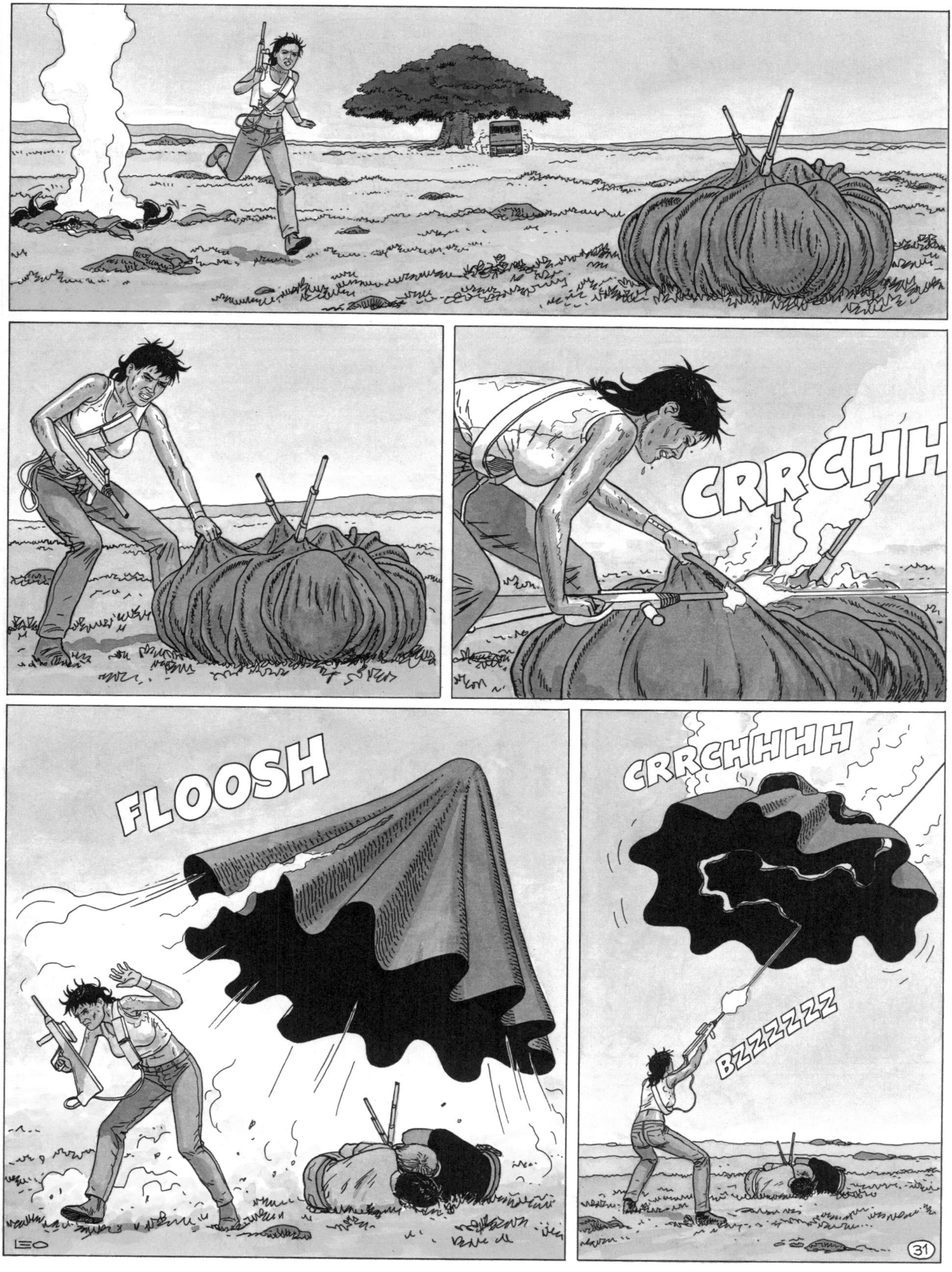
CRRCHH
FLOOSH
CRRCHHHH
BZZZZZZ
LEO
31

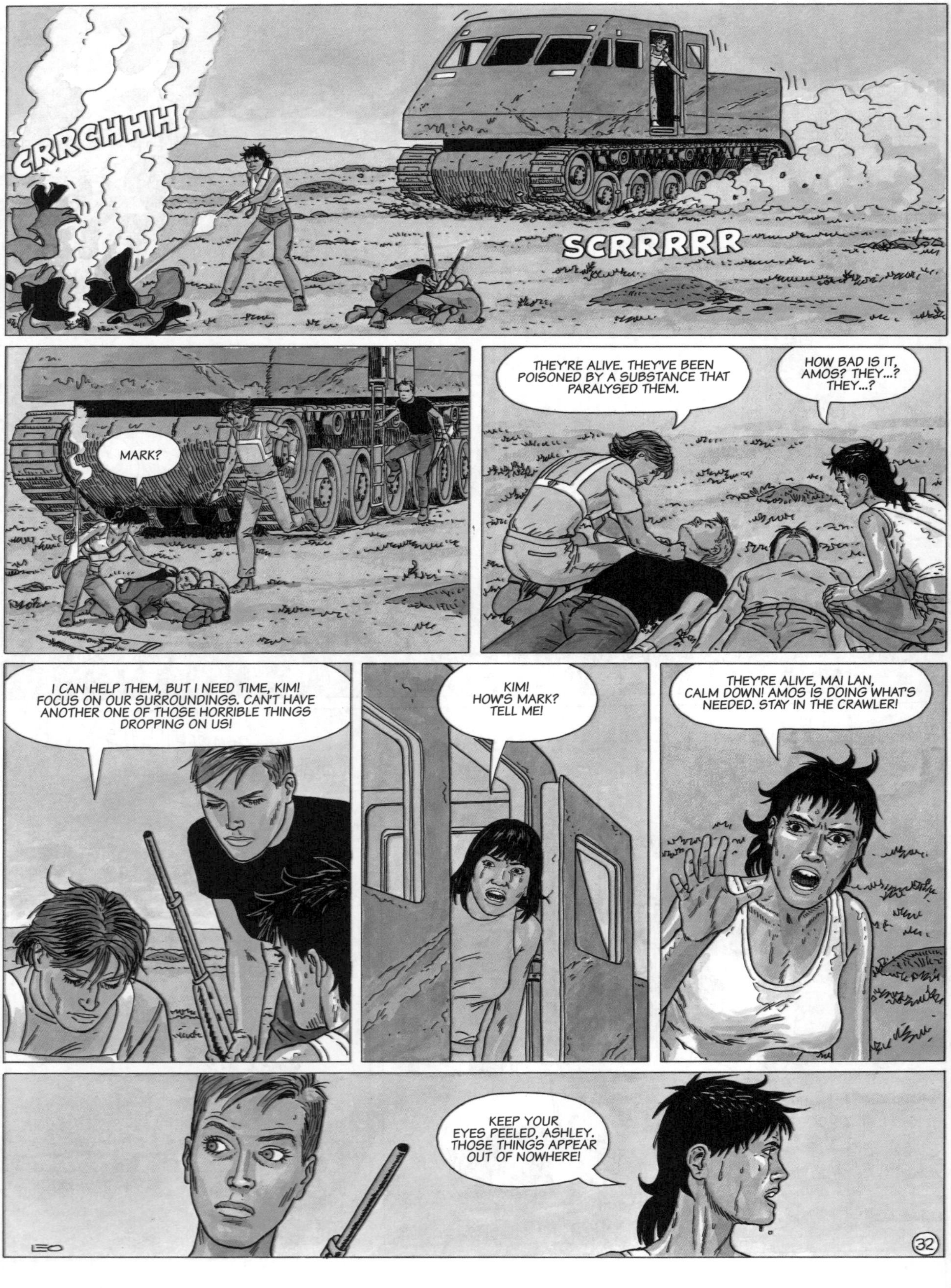
CRRCHHH
SCRRRRR
MARK?
THEY'RE ALIVE. THEY'VE BEEN POISONED BY A SUBSTANCE THAT PARALYSED THEM.
HOW BAD IS IT, AMOS? THEY...? THEY...?
I CAN HELP THEM, BUT I NEED TIME, KIM! FOCUS ON OUR SURROUNDINGS. CAN'T HAVE ANOTHER ONE OF THOSE HORRIBLE THINGS DROPPING ON US!
KIM! HOW'S MARK? TELL ME!
THEY'RE ALIVE, MAI LAN, CALM DOWN! AMOS IS DOING WHAT'S NEEDED. STAY IN THE CRAWLER!
KEEP YOUR EYES PEELED, ASHLEY. THOSE THINGS APPEAR OUT OF NOWHERE!
LEO
32

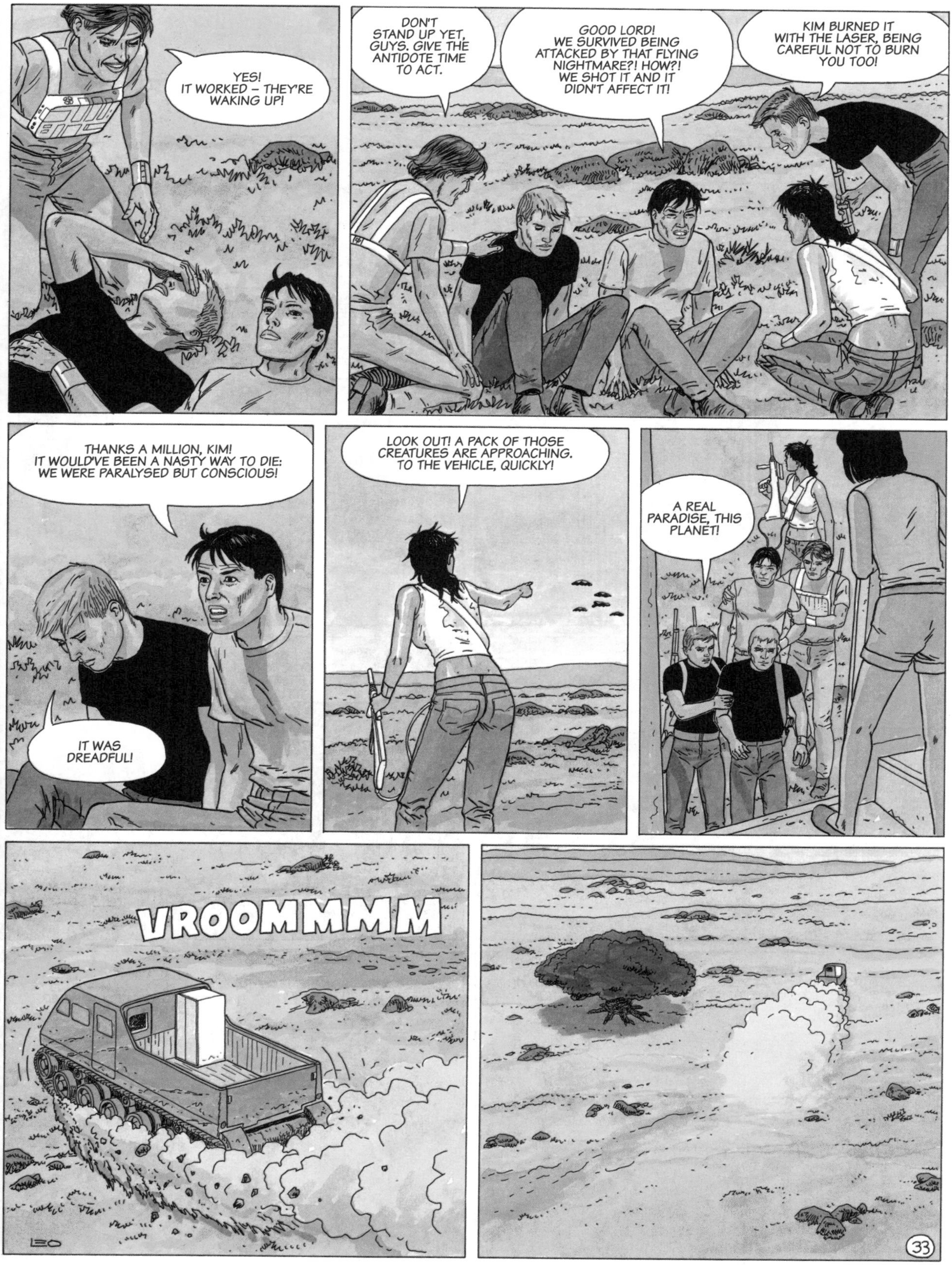
YES! IT WORKED – THEY'RE WAKING UP!
DON'T STAND UP YET, GUYS. GIVE THE ANTIDOTE TIME TO ACT.
GOOD LORD! WE SURVIVED BEING ATTACKED BY THAT FLYING NIGHTMARE?! HOW?! WE SHOT IT AND IT DIDN'T AFFECT IT!
KIM BURNED IT WITH THE LASER, BEING CAREFUL NOT TO BURN YOU TOO!
THANKS A MILLION, KIM! IT WOULD'VE BEEN A NASTY WAY TO DIE: WE WERE PARALYSED BUT CONSCIOUS!
IT WAS DREADFUL!
LOOK OUT! A PACK OF THOSE CREATURES ARE APPROACHING. TO THE VEHICLE, QUICKLY!
A REAL PARADISE, THIS PLANET!
VROOMMMM
LEO
33

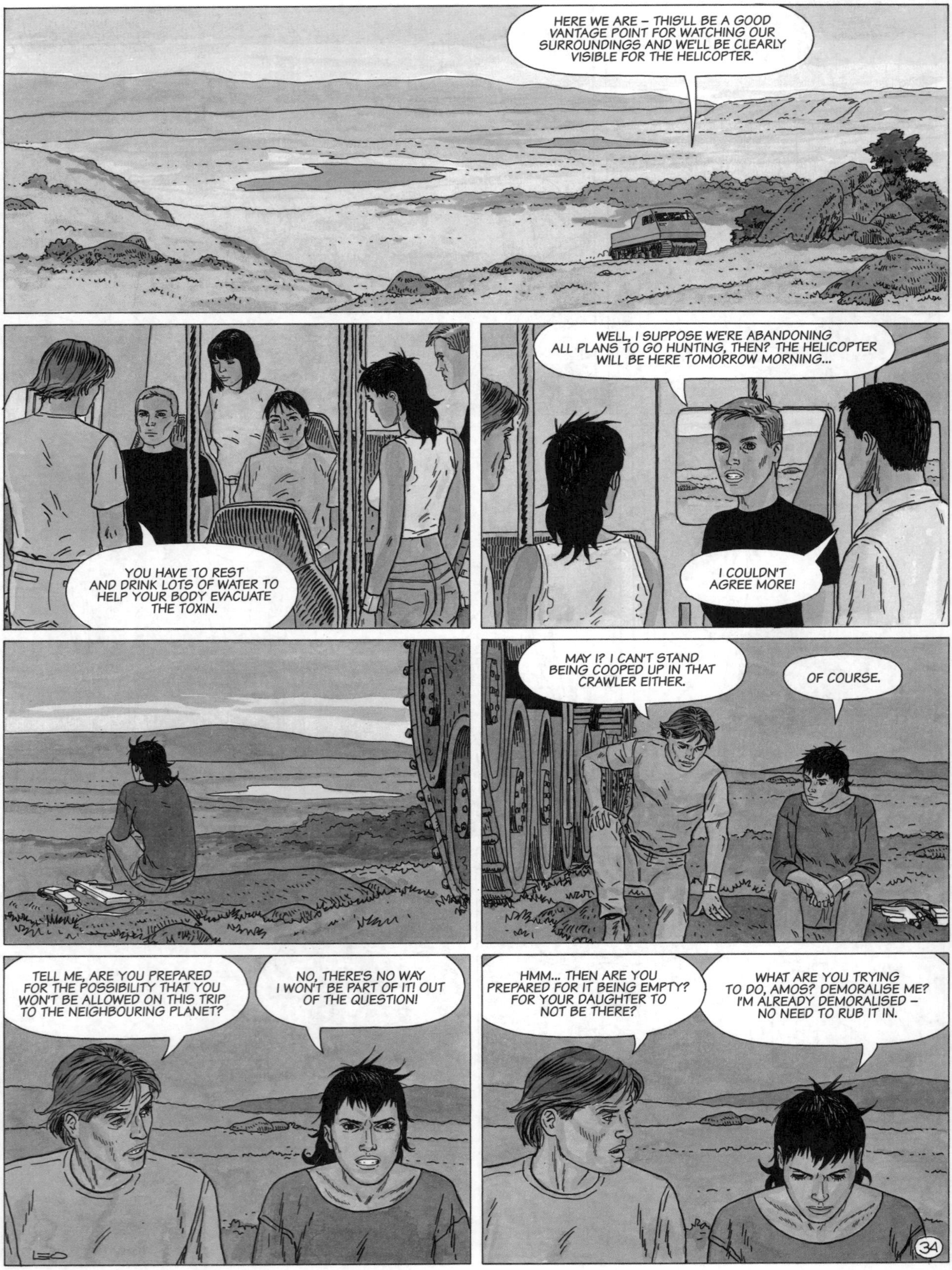
HERE WE ARE – THIS'LL BE A GOOD VANTAGE POINT FOR WATCHING OUR SURROUNDINGS AND WE'LL BE CLEARLY VISIBLE FOR THE HELICOPTER.
YOU HAVE TO REST AND DRINK LOTS OF WATER TO HELP YOUR BODY EVACUATE THE TOXIN.
WELL, I SUPPOSE WE'RE ABANDONING ALL PLANS TO GO HUNTING, THEN? THE HELICOPTER WILL BE HERE TOMORROW MORNING...
I COULDN'T AGREE MORE!
MAY I? I CAN'T STAND BEING COOPED UP IN THAT CRAWLER EITHER.
OF COURSE.
TELL ME, ARE YOU PREPARED FOR THE POSSIBILITY THAT YOU WON'T BE ALLOWED ON THIS TRIP TO THE NEIGHBOURING PLANET?
NO, THERE'S NO WAY I WON'T BE PART OF IT! OUT OF THE QUESTION!
LEO
HMM... THEN ARE YOU PREPARED FOR IT BEING EMPTY? FOR YOUR DAUGHTER TO NOT BE THERE?
WHAT ARE YOU TRYING TO DO, AMOS? DEMORALISE ME? I'M ALREADY DEMORALISED – NO NEED TO RUB IT IN.
34

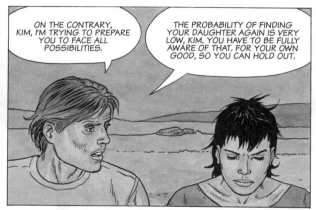

ON THE CONTRARY, KIM, I'M TRYING TO PREPARE YOU TO FACE ALL POSSIBILITIES.

THE PROBABILITY OF FINDING YOUR DAUGHTER AGAIN IS VERY LOW, KIM. YOU HAVE TO BE FULLY AWARE OF THAT. FOR YOUR OWN GOOD, SO YOU CAN HOLD OUT.

I AM AWARE, AMOS.

DON'T WORRY, I'M NOT GOING TO LOSE IT. AND I'LL GO THERE TO GET MY DAUGHTER. YOU'LL SEE.

ALL RIGHT.

AMOS...

MMM?

THAT KISS THE OTHER DAY... WHAT DID IT MEAN?

I JOINED THE ANTARES PROJECT TO GET AWAY FROM MY EX-WIFE AND TRY TO FORGET A BREAK-UP THAT WAS TOO PAINFUL. AND I'D PROMISED MYSELF NOT TO GET DRAWN INTO ANOTHER ROMANTIC EXPERIENCE FOR AT LEAST A CENTURY...

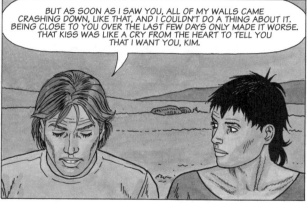

BUT AS SOON AS I SAW YOU, ALL OF MY WALLS CAME CRASHING DOWN, LIKE THAT, AND I COULDN'T DO A THING ABOUT IT. BEING CLOSE TO YOU OVER THE LAST FEW DAYS ONLY MADE IT WORSE. THAT KISS WAS LIKE A CRY FROM THE HEART TO TELL YOU THAT I WANT YOU, KIM.

BUT IT'S NEITHER THE TIME NOR THE PLACE TO DISCUSS THIS... I'M GOING BACK IN. IT'S GETTING COLD.

35

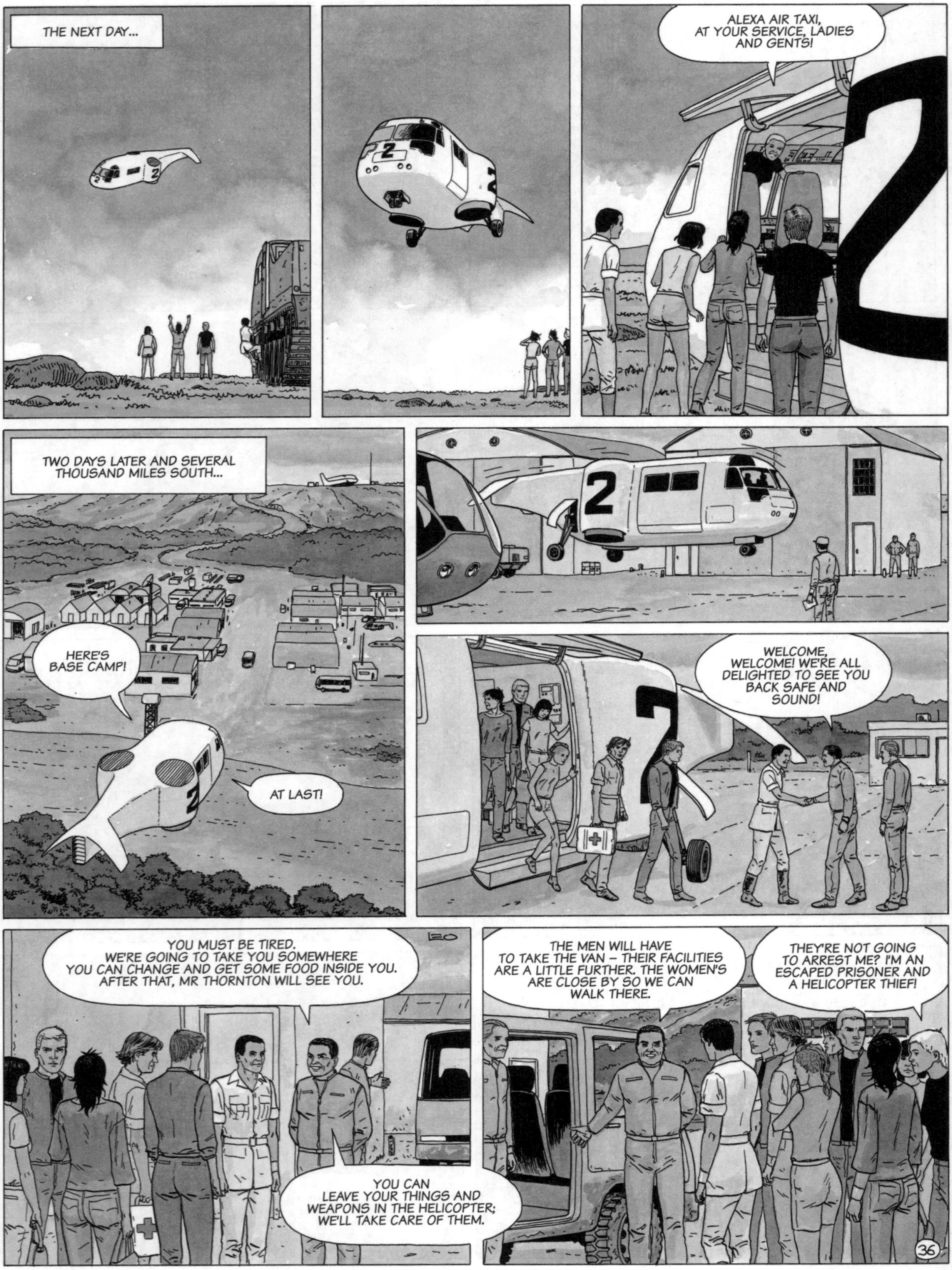
THE NEXT DAY...
ALEXA AIR TAXI, AT YOUR SERVICE, LADIES AND GENTS!
TWO DAYS LATER AND SEVERAL THOUSAND MILES SOUTH...
HERE'S BASE CAMP!
AT LAST!
WELCOME, WELCOME! WE'RE ALL DELIGHTED TO SEE YOU BACK SAFE AND SOUND!
YOU MUST BE TIRED. WE'RE GOING TO TAKE YOU SOMEWHERE YOU CAN CHANGE AND GET SOME FOOD INSIDE YOU. AFTER THAT, MR THORNTON WILL SEE YOU.
YOU CAN LEAVE YOUR THINGS AND WEAPONS IN THE HELICOPTER; WE'LL TAKE CARE OF THEM.
THE MEN WILL HAVE TO TAKE THE VAN – THEIR FACILITIES ARE A LITTLE FURTHER. THE WOMEN'S ARE CLOSE BY SO WE CAN WALK THERE.
THEY'RE NOT GOING TO ARREST ME? I'M AN ESCAPED PRISONER AND A HELICOPTER THIEF!
36

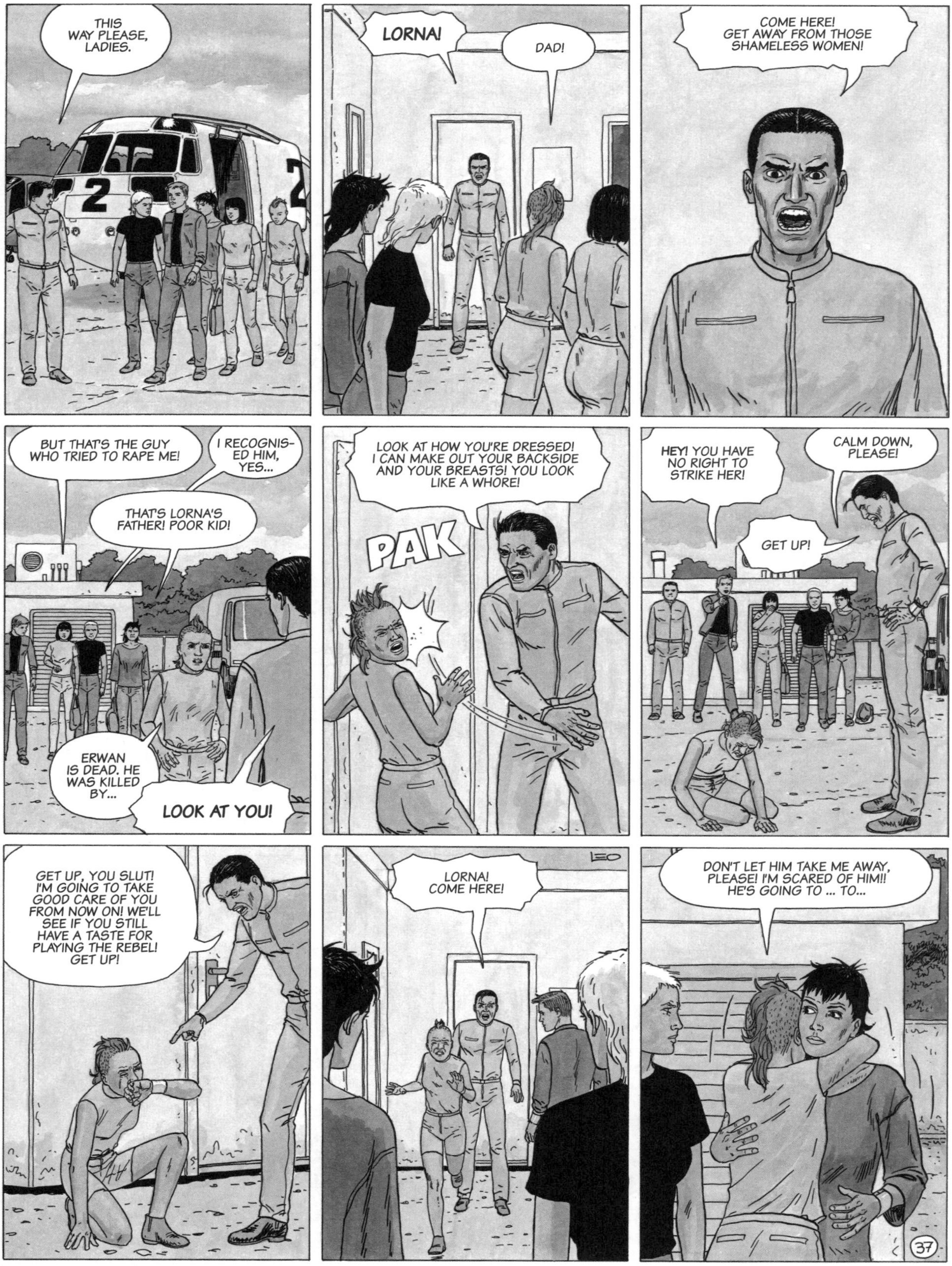
THIS WAY PLEASE, LADIES.
LORNA!
DAD!
COME HERE! GET AWAY FROM THOSE SHAMELESS WOMEN!
BUT THAT'S THE GUY WHO TRIED TO RAPE ME!
I RECOGNISED HIM, YES...
THAT'S LORNA'S FATHER! POOR KID!
ERWAN IS DEAD. HE WAS KILLED BY...
LOOK AT YOU!
LOOK AT HOW YOU'RE DRESSED! I CAN MAKE OUT YOUR BACKSIDE AND YOUR BREASTS! YOU LOOK LIKE A WHORE!
PAK
HEY! YOU HAVE NO RIGHT TO STRIKE HER!
CALM DOWN, PLEASE!
GET UP!
GET UP, YOU SLUT! I'M GOING TO TAKE GOOD CARE OF YOU FROM NOW ON! WE'LL SEE IF YOU STILL HAVE A TASTE FOR PLAYING THE REBEL! GET UP!
LEO
LORNA! COME HERE!
DON'T LET HIM TAKE ME AWAY, PLEASE! I'M SCARED OF HIM!! HE'S GOING TO ... TO...
37

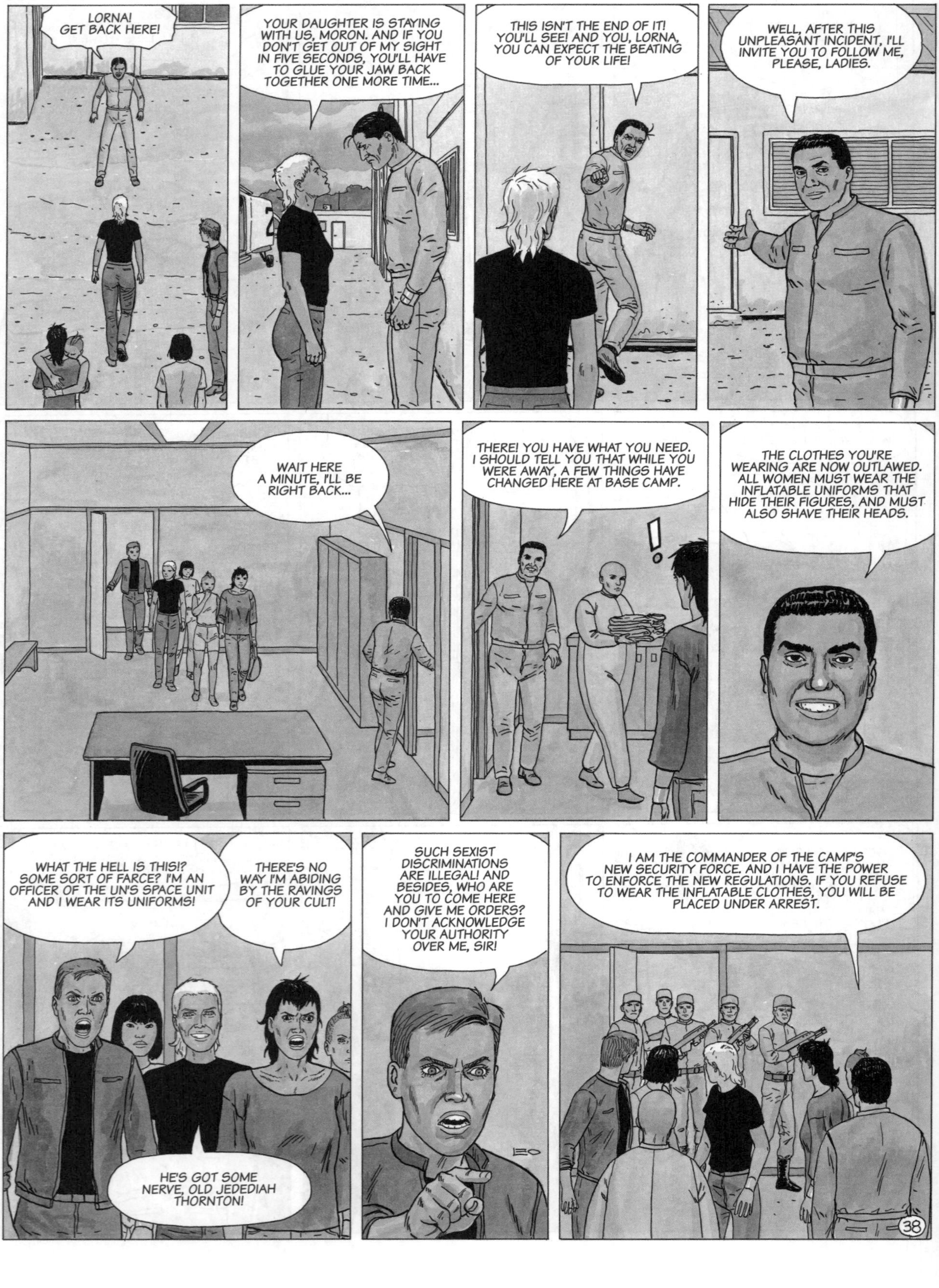
LORNA! GET BACK HERE!
YOUR DAUGHTER IS STAYING WITH US, MORON. AND IF YOU DON'T GET OUT OF MY SIGHT IN FIVE SECONDS, YOU'LL HAVE TO GLUE YOUR JAW BACK TOGETHER ONE MORE TIME...
THIS ISN'T THE END OF IT! YOU'LL SEE! AND YOU, LORNA, YOU CAN EXPECT THE BEATING OF YOUR LIFE!
WELL, AFTER THIS UNPLEASANT INCIDENT, I'LL INVITE YOU TO FOLLOW ME, PLEASE, LADIES.
WAIT HERE A MINUTE, I'LL BE RIGHT BACK...
THERE! YOU HAVE WHAT YOU NEED. I SHOULD TELL YOU THAT WHILE YOU WERE AWAY, A FEW THINGS HAVE CHANGED HERE AT BASE CAMP.
!
THE CLOTHES YOU'RE WEARING ARE NOW OUTLAWED. ALL WOMEN MUST WEAR THE INFLATABLE UNIFORMS THAT HIDE THEIR FIGURES, AND MUST ALSO SHAVE THEIR HEADS.
WHAT THE HELL IS THIS!? SOME SORT OF FARCE? I'M AN OFFICER OF THE UN'S SPACE UNIT AND I WEAR ITS UNIFORMS!
THERE'S NO WAY I'M ABIDING BY THE RAVINGS OF YOUR CULT!
HE'S GOT SOME NERVE, OLD JEDEDIAH THORNTON!
SUCH SEXIST DISCRIMINATIONS ARE ILLEGAL! AND BESIDES, WHO ARE YOU TO COME HERE AND GIVE ME ORDERS? I DON'T ACKNOWLEDGE YOUR AUTHORITY OVER ME, SIR!
LEO
I AM THE COMMANDER OF THE CAMP'S NEW SECURITY FORCE. AND I HAVE THE POWER TO ENFORCE THE NEW REGULATIONS. IF YOU REFUSE TO WEAR THE INFLATABLE CLOTHES, YOU WILL BE PLACED UNDER ARREST.
38

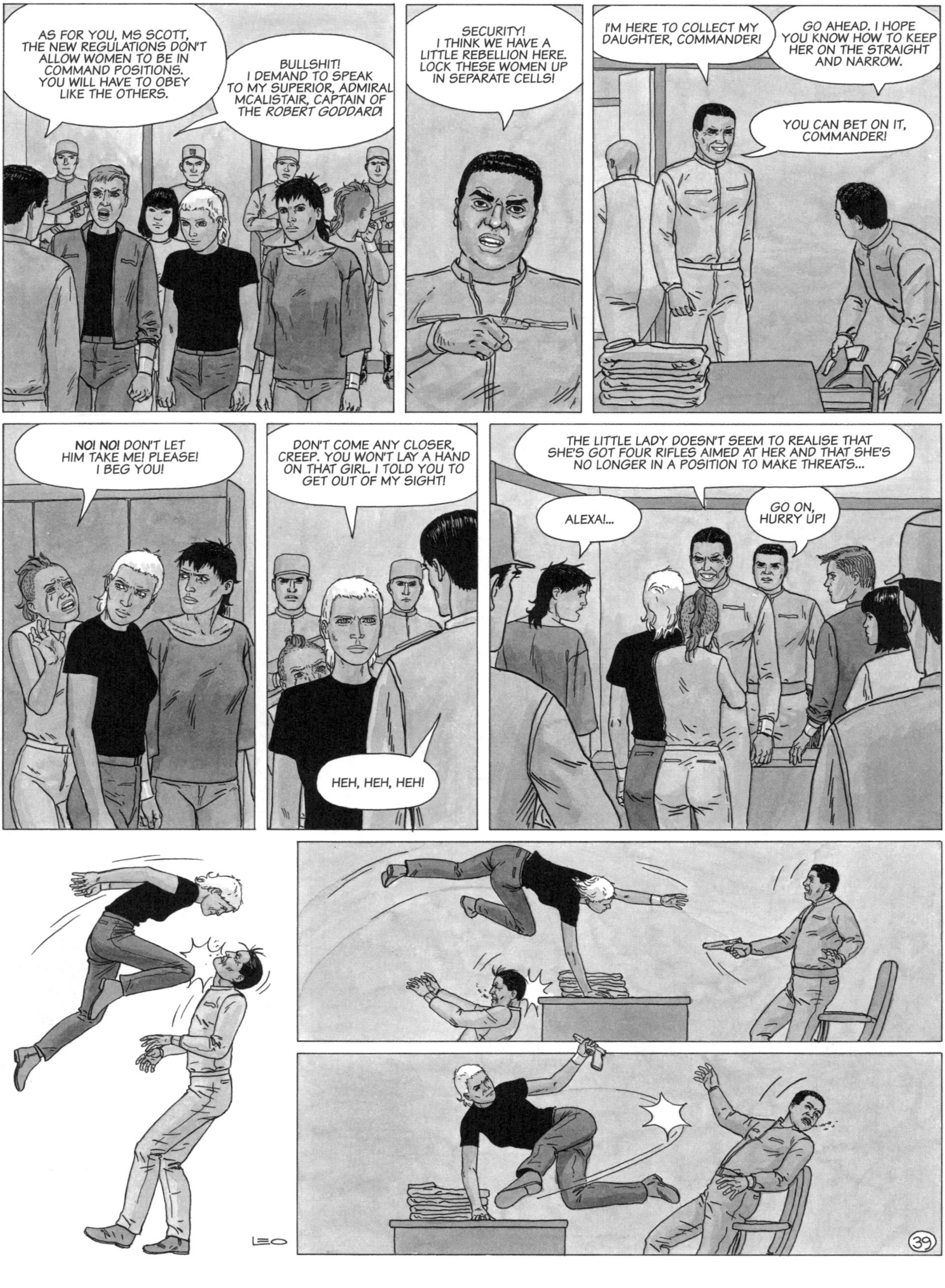

AS FOR YOU, MS SCOTT, THE NEW REGULATIONS DON'T ALLOW WOMEN TO BE IN COMMAND POSITIONS. YOU WILL HAVE TO OBEY LIKE THE OTHERS.
BULLSHIT! I DEMAND TO SPEAK TO MY SUPERIOR, ADMIRAL MCALISTAIR, CAPTAIN OF THE *ROBERT GODDARD*!
SECURITY! I THINK WE HAVE A LITTLE REBELLION HERE. LOCK THESE WOMEN UP IN SEPARATE CELLS!
I'M HERE TO COLLECT MY DAUGHTER, COMMANDER!
GO AHEAD. I HOPE YOU KNOW HOW TO KEEP HER ON THE STRAIGHT AND NARROW.
YOU CAN BET ON IT, COMMANDER!
NO! NO! DON'T LET HIM TAKE ME! PLEASE! I BEG YOU!
DON'T COME ANY CLOSER, CREEP. YOU WON'T LAY A HAND ON THAT GIRL. I TOLD YOU TO GET OUT OF MY SIGHT!
HEH, HEH, HEH!
THE LITTLE LADY DOESN'T SEEM TO REALISE THAT SHE'S GOT FOUR RIFLES AIMED AT HER AND THAT SHE'S NO LONGER IN A POSITION TO MAKE THREATS...
ALEXA!...
GO ON, HURRY UP!
LEO
39

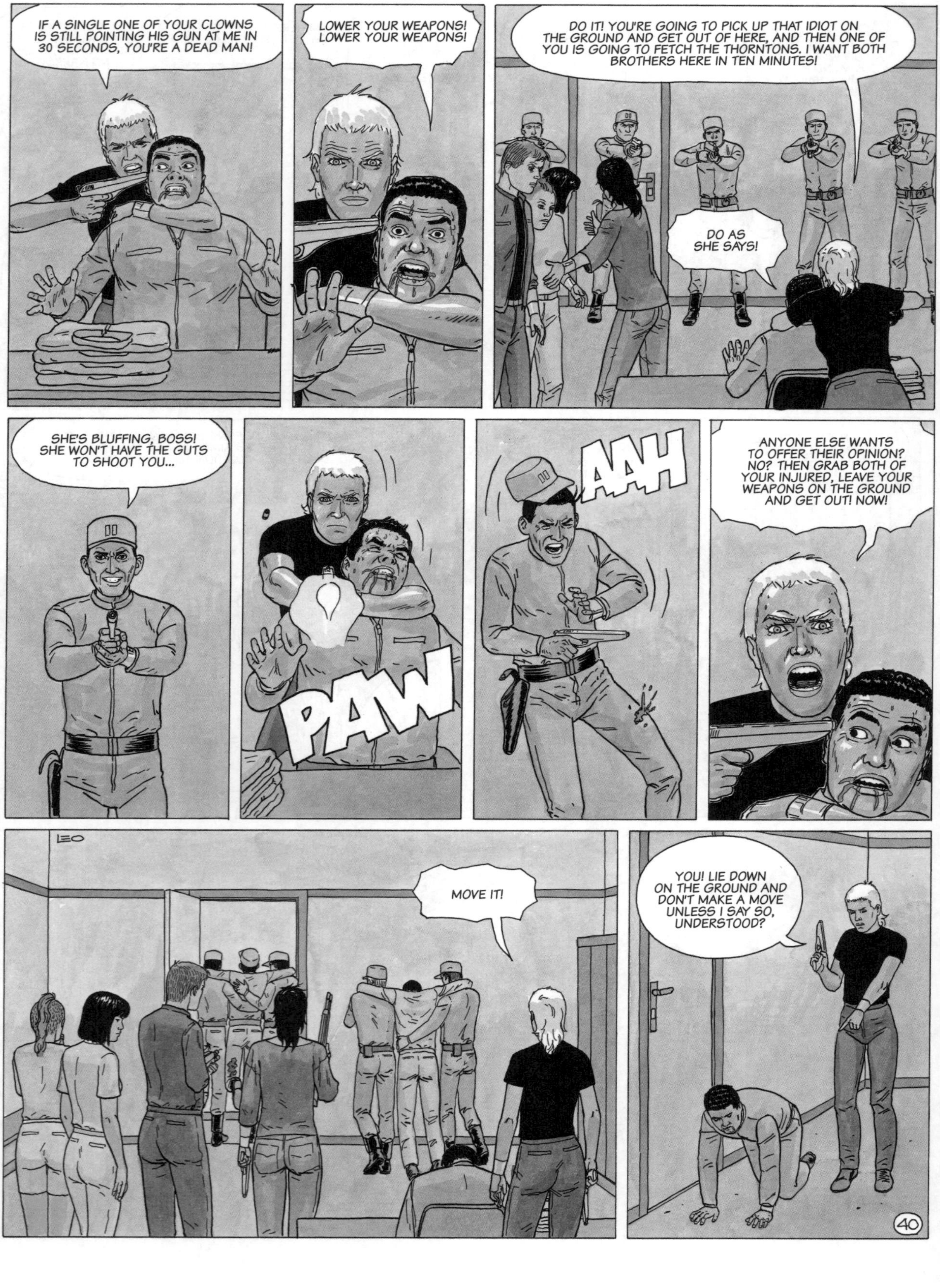
IF A SINGLE ONE OF YOUR CLOWNS IS STILL POINTING HIS GUN AT ME IN 30 SECONDS, YOU'RE A DEAD MAN!
LOWER YOUR WEAPONS! LOWER YOUR WEAPONS!
DO IT! YOU'RE GOING TO PICK UP THAT IDIOT ON THE GROUND AND GET OUT OF HERE, AND THEN ONE OF YOU IS GOING TO FETCH THE THORNTONS. I WANT BOTH BROTHERS HERE IN TEN MINUTES!
DO AS SHE SAYS!
SHE'S BLUFFING, BOSS! SHE WON'T HAVE THE GUTS TO SHOOT YOU...
PAW
AAH
ANYONE ELSE WANTS TO OFFER THEIR OPINION? NO? THEN GRAB BOTH OF YOUR INJURED, LEAVE YOUR WEAPONS ON THE GROUND AND GET OUT! NOW!
LEO
MOVE IT!
YOU! LIE DOWN ON THE GROUND AND DON'T MAKE A MOVE UNLESS I SAY SO, UNDERSTOOD?
40

SUCH EFFICIENCY, MA'AM! BUT SUCH A VIOLENT OUTBURST! I'M IN SHOCK!

ME TOO, SCOTT, ME TOO! BUT I'VE HAD ENOUGH OF THOSE ARROGANT IMBECILES' AGGRESSION. THEY KEEP TRYING TO IMPOSE THEIR OWN MEDIOCRITY ON OTHERS, ESPECIALLY WOMEN, AND I CAN'T STAND IT ANY MORE, DAMMIT!

HMM... BE THAT AS IT MAY, YOU BESTED SIX FULLY ARMED MEN – I STILL CAN'T BELIEVE IT!

DON'T FORGET I'M 141, SCOTT. I'VE HAD TIME TO LEARN A PIROUETTE OR TWO.

DO YOU THINK THE TWO THORNTONS WILL COME?

NO IDEA. BUT I FIGURED...

JEDEDIAH THORNTON IS NO LONGER ON THE PLANET. HE WENT UP INTO ORBIT AND HE MUST BE ON HIS WAY TO ANTARES 4 BY NOW.

THE MISSION'S LEFT ALREADY?! YOU'RE LYING!

I'M NOT LYING. THEY MOVED THE DEPARTURE FORWARD.

THOSE BASTARDS! I HAD TO BE ON THAT SHIP! I HAD TO! MY DAUGHTER... SHE...

WE'LL FIND A WAY, KIM. WE'LL MAKE ANOTHER TRIP.

I'M AFRAID THAT WON'T BE POSSIBLE, MA'AM. WE DIDN'T BRING ENOUGH FUEL FOR ANOTHER CROSSING.

I'M GOING TO KILL THAT IDIOT JEDEDIAH THORNTON! I'M GOING TO KILL THAT FUCKER WITH MY BARE HANDS!

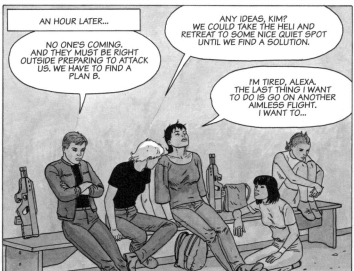

AN HOUR LATER...

NO ONE'S COMING. AND THEY MUST BE RIGHT OUTSIDE PREPARING TO ATTACK US. WE HAVE TO FIND A PLAN B.

ANY IDEAS, KIM? WE COULD TAKE THE HELI AND RETREAT TO SOME NICE QUIET SPOT UNTIL WE FIND A SOLUTION.

I'M TIRED, ALEXA. THE LAST THING I WANT TO DO IS GO ON ANOTHER AIMLESS FLIGHT. I WANT TO...

SOMEONE'S COMING!

HEY! IT'S ME, PAD! WE'RE COMING IN – DON'T GO SHOOTING AT US, NOW!

LEO

41

HELLO THERE! I BRING GOOD NEWS!

THE GOOD GUYS WON AND THE BAD GUYS HAVE BEEN ARRESTED, JUST LIKE IN THE SUNDAY MOVIES! HEH, HEH, HEH!

IT'S THE TRIP TO ANTARES 4 THAT TRIGGERED EVERYTHING...

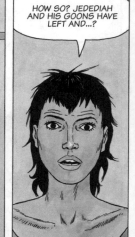

HOW SO? JEDEDIAH AND HIS GOONS HAVE LEFT AND...?

THEY HAVEN'T LEFT! THE ASTRONAUT OFFICERS REFUSED TO MAKE THE TRIP WITHOUT YOU LOT!

WHAT?!

YEP! THEY SAID THERE COULD BE SOME HIGHLY ADVANCED BEINGS OVER THERE ON ANTARES 4, AND THERE WAS NO WAY IN HELL THEY'D LET THAT QUARTET OF BACKWARD-THINKING FANATICS REPRESENT MANKIND!

OH, IT'S SO GOOD TO HEAR THAT, MY FRIENDS! SUCH A RELIEF!

MEANWHILE, WE ORGANISED THE RESISTANCE DOWN HERE. LOADS OF PEOPLE WERE UNHAPPY WITH THE MESSIANIC DRIFT OF THE ANTARES PROJECT AND ITS PRIMITIVE, ABSURD NEW REGULATIONS. ONCE THE POLICE CAME OVER TO OUR SIDE, EVERYTHING HAPPENED FAST AND WE QUICKLY GAINED THE UPPER HAND.

THE POLICE HELPED YOU?!

WE'RE PART OF THE UN SPACE UNIT. OUR DUTY IS TO UPHOLD THE LAW APPROVED BY THE UNO, NOT THE INTERESTS OF A PROJECT'S SPONSORS.

I'M GLAD TO SEE YOU BACK IN UNIFORM, NORA HUTTON.

I OWE IT IN LARGE PART TO YOU AND YOUR FRIENDS, MA'AM.

42

TWO DAYS LATER...

SO? WHAT'S BEEN DECIDED?

BAD NEWS? YOU DON'T LOOK VERY HAPPY...

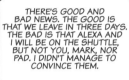

THERE'S GOOD AND BAD NEWS. THE GOOD IS THAT WE LEAVE IN THREE DAYS. THE BAD IS THAT ALEXA AND I WILL BE ON THE SHUTTLE, BUT NOT YOU, MARK, NOR PAD. I DIDN'T MANAGE TO CONVINCE THEM.

THEY SAY WE NEED TWO PILOTS: IT'LL BE ALEXA AND ASHLEY SCOTT, WITH ZAO AS A BACKUP. THEY DIDN'T CONSIDER IT NECESSARY TO ADD A FOURTH.

THAT'S HARD TO SWALLOW! NOT BEING ABLE TO BE WITH YOU OVER THERE... ESPECIALLY YOU, KIM! I... I...

YES, IT'S TOUGH FOR ME TOO. BUT I JUST COULDN'T CHANGE THEIR MINDS. I'M SORRY.

BUT THERE'S MORE BAD NEWS. REALLY BAD...

JEDEDIAH THORNTON WILL BE COMING ALONG.

WHAT?!

BLIMEY!

WHY?! I DON'T UNDERSTAND!

OH, ALEXA, IF YOU KNEW HOW HARD I FOUGHT AGAINST THAT DECISION! ZAO AND ASHLEY TOO. BUT NOTHING WORKED. THERE WAS A LOT OF NEGOTIATING BETWEEN THE ADMIRAL, THE UN REPRESENTATIVE, THE HEAD OF THE LEGAL DEPARTMENT...

THE BOTTOM LINE IS THAT "FORWARD ENTERPRISES" IS THE OWNER OF THE ANTARES PROJECT, WHICH GIVES IT INESCAPABLE, INALIENABLE RIGHTS. THEY HAVE THE RIGHT TO INCLUDE A REPRESENTATIVE OF THEIR GROUP IN THE MISSION.

AND ELIJAH THORNTON, THE BIG BOSS, CHOSE HIS BROTHER JEDEDIAH.

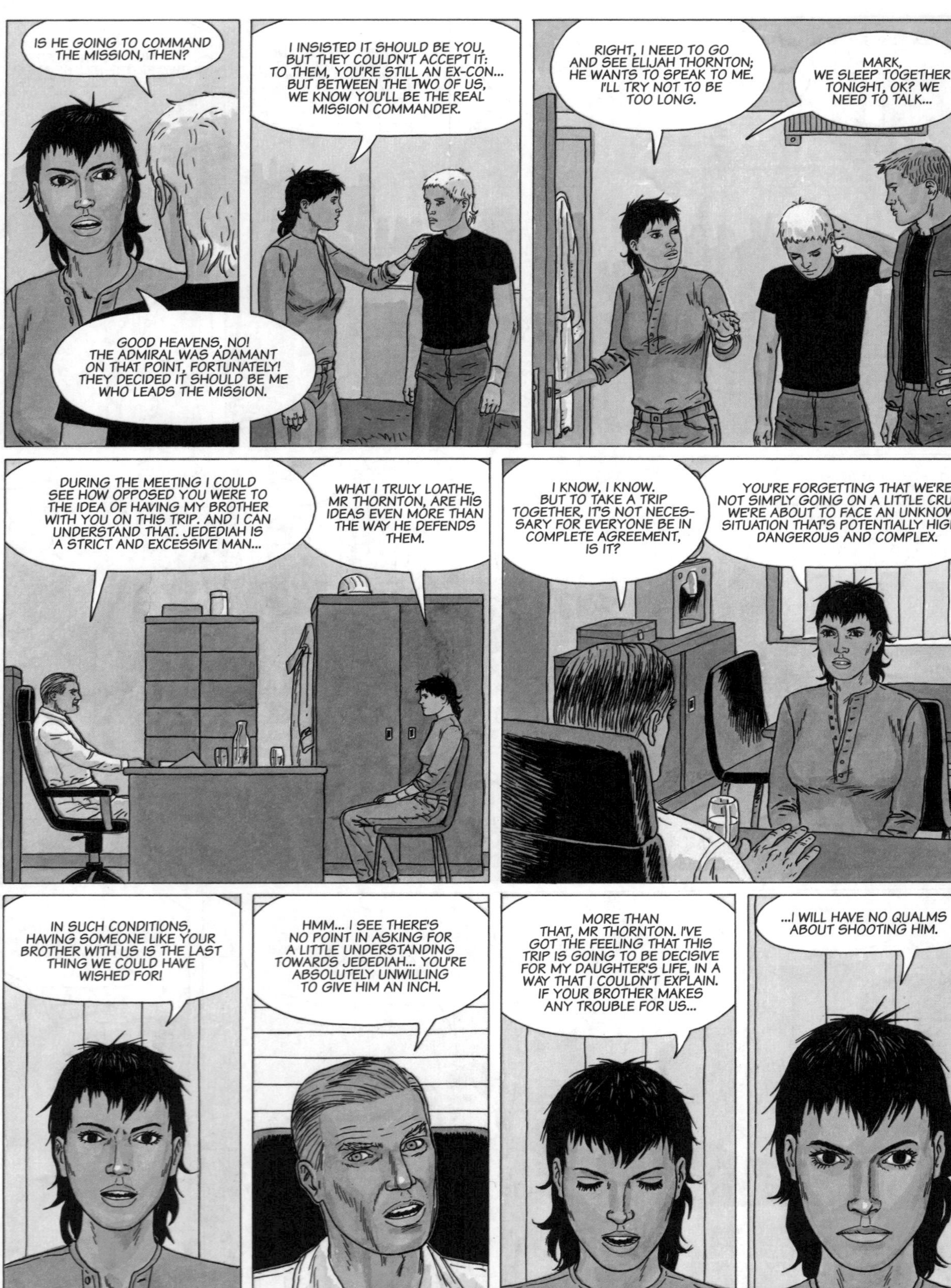
IS HE GOING TO COMMAND THE MISSION, THEN?
GOOD HEAVENS, NO! THE ADMIRAL WAS ADAMANT ON THAT POINT, FORTUNATELY! THEY DECIDED IT SHOULD BE ME WHO LEADS THE MISSION.
I INSISTED IT SHOULD BE YOU, BUT THEY COULDN'T ACCEPT IT: TO THEM, YOU'RE STILL AN EX-CON... BUT BETWEEN THE TWO OF US, WE KNOW YOU'LL BE THE REAL MISSION COMMANDER.
RIGHT, I NEED TO GO AND SEE ELIJAH THORNTON; HE WANTS TO SPEAK TO ME. I'LL TRY NOT TO BE TOO LONG.
MARK, WE SLEEP TOGETHER TONIGHT, OK? WE NEED TO TALK...
DURING THE MEETING I COULD SEE HOW OPPOSED YOU WERE TO THE IDEA OF HAVING MY BROTHER WITH YOU ON THIS TRIP. AND I CAN UNDERSTAND THAT. JEDEDIAH IS A STRICT AND EXCESSIVE MAN...
WHAT I TRULY LOATHE, MR THORNTON, ARE HIS IDEAS EVEN MORE THAN THE WAY HE DEFENDS THEM.
I KNOW, I KNOW. BUT TO TAKE A TRIP TOGETHER, IT'S NOT NECES-SARY FOR EVERYONE BE IN COMPLETE AGREEMENT, IS IT?
YOU'RE FORGETTING THAT WE'RE NOT SIMPLY GOING ON A LITTLE CRUISE. WE'RE ABOUT TO FACE AN UNKNOWN SITUATION THAT'S POTENTIALLY HIGHLY DANGEROUS AND COMPLEX.
IN SUCH CONDITIONS, HAVING SOMEONE LIKE YOUR BROTHER WITH US IS THE LAST THING WE COULD HAVE WISHED FOR!
HMM... I SEE THERE'S NO POINT IN ASKING FOR A LITTLE UNDERSTANDING TOWARDS JEDEDIAH... YOU'RE ABSOLUTELY UNWILLING TO GIVE HIM AN INCH.
MORE THAN THAT, MR THORNTON. I'VE GOT THE FEELING THAT THIS TRIP IS GOING TO BE DECISIVE FOR MY DAUGHTER'S LIFE, IN A WAY THAT I COULDN'T EXPLAIN. IF YOUR BROTHER MAKES ANY TROUBLE FOR US...
...I WILL HAVE NO QUALMS ABOUT SHOOTING HIM.
LEO
44

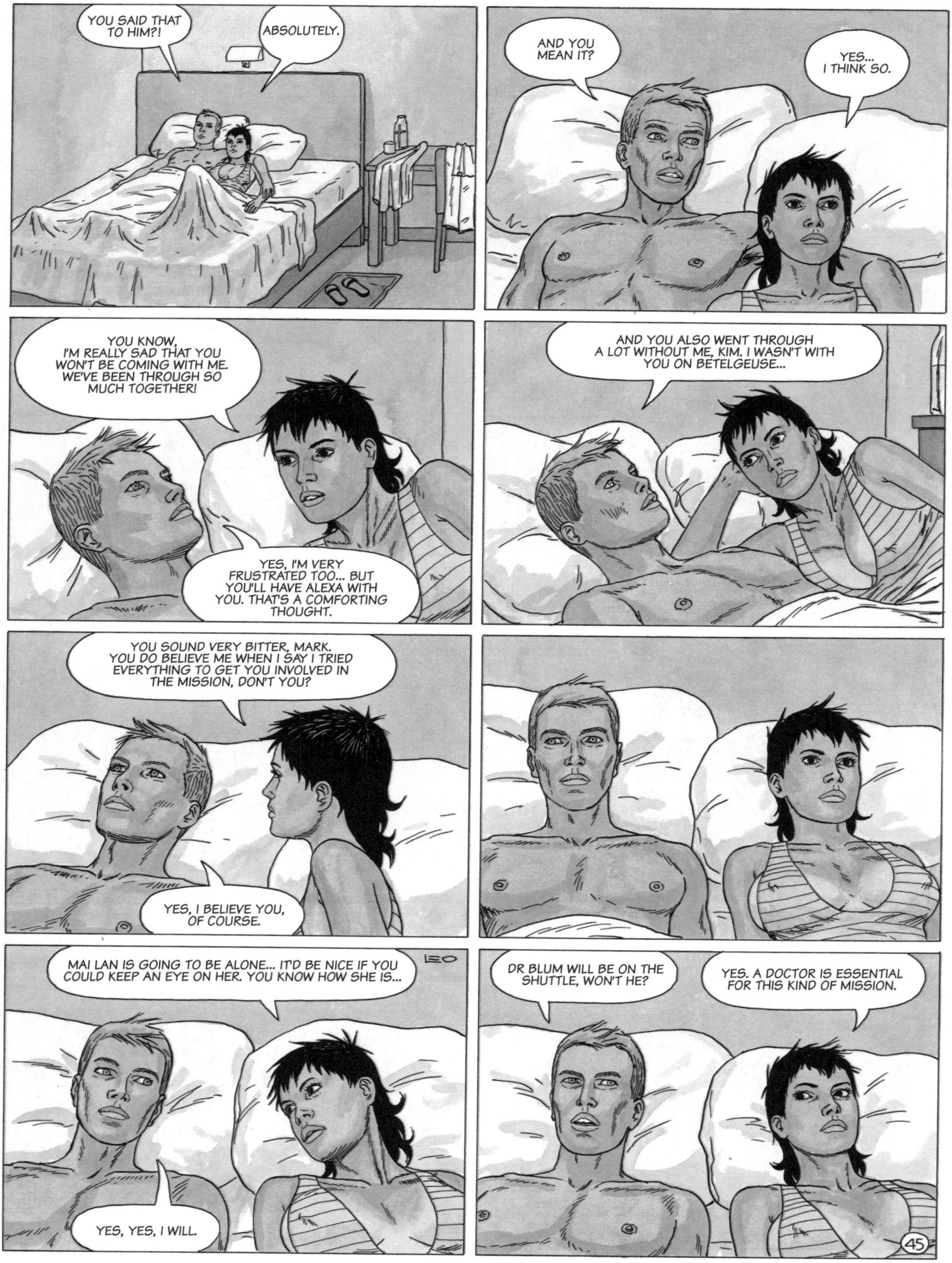
YOU SAID THAT TO HIM?!
ABSOLUTELY.
AND YOU MEAN IT?
YES... I THINK SO.
YOU KNOW, I'M REALLY SAD THAT YOU WON'T BE COMING WITH ME. WE'VE BEEN THROUGH SO MUCH TOGETHER!
YES, I'M VERY FRUSTRATED TOO... BUT YOU'LL HAVE ALEXA WITH YOU. THAT'S A COMFORTING THOUGHT.
AND YOU ALSO WENT THROUGH A LOT WITHOUT ME, KIM. I WASN'T WITH YOU ON BETELGEUSE...
YOU SOUND VERY BITTER, MARK. YOU DO BELIEVE ME WHEN I SAY I TRIED EVERYTHING TO GET YOU INVOLVED IN THE MISSION, DON'T YOU?
YES, I BELIEVE YOU, OF COURSE.
MAI LAN IS GOING TO BE ALONE... IT'D BE NICE IF YOU COULD KEEP AN EYE ON HER. YOU KNOW HOW SHE IS...
LEO
YES, YES, I WILL.
DR BLUM WILL BE ON THE SHUTTLE, WON'T HE?
YES. A DOCTOR IS ESSENTIAL FOR THIS KIND OF MISSION.
45

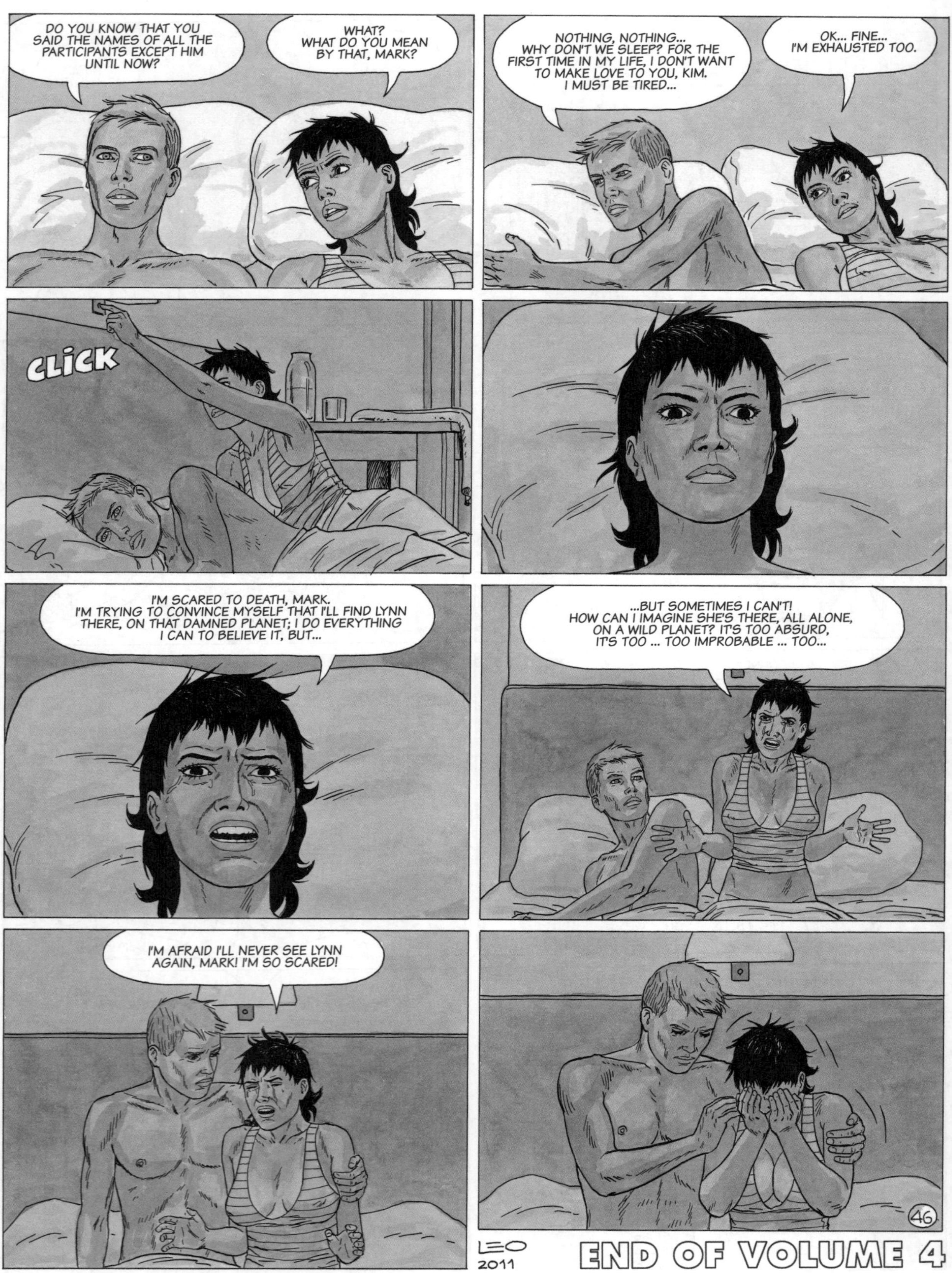
DO YOU KNOW THAT YOU SAID THE NAMES OF ALL THE PARTICIPANTS EXCEPT HIM UNTIL NOW?
WHAT? WHAT DO YOU MEAN BY THAT, MARK?
NOTHING, NOTHING... WHY DON'T WE SLEEP? FOR THE FIRST TIME IN MY LIFE, I DON'T WANT TO MAKE LOVE TO YOU, KIM. I MUST BE TIRED...
OK... FINE... I'M EXHAUSTED TOO.
CLICK
I'M SCARED TO DEATH, MARK. I'M TRYING TO CONVINCE MYSELF THAT I'LL FIND LYNN THERE, ON THAT DAMNED PLANET; I DO EVERYTHING I CAN TO BELIEVE IT, BUT...
...BUT SOMETIMES I CAN'T! HOW CAN I IMAGINE SHE'S THERE, ALL ALONE, ON A WILD PLANET? IT'S TOO ABSURD, IT'S TOO ... TOO IMPROBABLE ... TOO...
I'M AFRAID I'LL NEVER SEE LYNN AGAIN, MARK! I'M SO SCARED!
46
LEO 2011
END OF VOLUME 4